S0-BEI-202

THE
Triumphant
Church

A three-part study

from the writings of

Richard Wurmbrand,

John Piper, &

Milton Martin

Compiled by The Voice of the Martyrs

Compiled by:
THE VOICE OF THE MARTYRS
P.O. Box 443
Bartlesville, OK 74005-0443
(918) 337-8015

Contents

Preparing
for the
Underground
Church

Pastor Richard Wurmbrand

© 1999 by The Voice of the Martyrs.

For more information on today's persecuted church and how you can help, contact:

The Voice of the Martyrs, Inc.
P.O. Box 443
Bartlesville, OK 74005
(918) 337-8015
the voice@vom-usa.org
www.persecution.com

Foreword

CONTRARY TO WHAT one might think, this is not a kind of mini-manual on the organization of some clandestine Christian society called the Underground Church. It is simply a forward look at the Church by one whose pastoral life, prison experiences, and extensive preaching ministries have done so much to alert the world to the dangers of atheistic communism.

Richard Wurmbrand's writings need no introduction. They are forthright and penetrating, seldom leaving the reader indifferent to the message they proclaim. Little attempt has been made to edit this manuscript. Some of the expressions used are characteristic of the man who thinks as a Hebrew, reads as a linguist, prays like an apostle, and writes like a prophet. The message is crystal clear.

If what some Christian leaders are saying is true, then sooner or later the Church must face two alternatives: sociopolitical compromise with anti-Christian forces or incur the wrath of a controlled political-religious hierarchy. In that case, Wurmbrand is right—*We must prepare now.*

Since these alternatives have already been posed in many parts of the world, there is no reason to believe that the area where we live will continue to escape their realities. Let us then, as Christians, prepare ourselves now and be sure that our children have a clear example before them if their turn comes.

THE PUBLISHER

Prepare for the Underground Church—Now

"THEN ANANIAS ANSWERED, 'Lord, I have heard from many about this man, how much harm he has done to Your saints in Jerusalem.' But the Lord said to him, 'Go, for he is a chosen vessel of Mine to bear My name before Gentiles, kings, and the children of Israel. *For I will show him how many things he must suffer for My name's sake'*" (Acts 9:13,15,16).

To my knowledge, there exists not one single theological seminary, Bible school, or university in the whole world that has a course on the Underground Church. You may learn in seminaries about Sebalianism and Apollinarianism. Five minutes after you have finished the seminary, you forget about them. You probably will never meet a Sabelian or an Apollinarian. We learn about the Coptic Church and about all kinds of small sects that we might never meet in our life. The Church underground is the Church of one-third of the world, men who had never thought before that they would have to belong to an underground church. While America was preoccupied with Watergate, Communists took over fifteen countries. Islam and Humanism are gaining influence and power. Christian pastors must know what an underground church looks like and what it does. I spoke with a bishop in Britain for an hour or so about underground church work. Finally, he said, "Excuse me, but you speak of my hobby; I am very interested in church architecture. Would you please tell me if the underground churches use Gothic styles in the building of churches?"

If I would tell you who this bishop is, you could not bear even to imagine how a man with so great a name could ask such a question.

The Underground Church is comparatively unknown. We have it right next-door, but we are not ready to join it and we are not trained for it. Every Christian pastor now has the whole world as his parish and we must know this because we might pass through tragic circumstances. Even if we do not pass through these tragic circumstances we have a duty to help and to instruct those who do pass through them.

In Muslim nations, in Red China and so on, many believers have become victims. Many have gone into prisons and many have died in prison. We cannot be proud of this. The better thing would have been to be so well instructed on how to do underground work and not to be captured.

In a war, those who die for their fatherland are not admired as much as the heroes who make the enemy die for *their* fatherland. It is not *I* who should die for *my* fatherland; *he* should die for *his*. I admire those who know how to work so well that they are not caught. We have to know the underground work.

Preparing for Suffering

Suffering cannot be avoided in the Underground Church, whatever measures are taken, but suffering should be reduced to the minimum.

It is not possible to give a course on the Church underground in a short time. I would urge you to ask your synod or denomination to introduce courses on the Underground Church.

What happens in a country when oppressive powers take over? In some countries the terror started at once, as in Mozambique and Cambodia. In other places religious liberty follows as never before. And so it begins. Some regimes come to power without having real power. They do not have the people on their side. They have not necessarily organized their police and their staff of the army yet. In Russia, the Communists immediately gave great liberty to the Protestants in order to destroy the Orthodox. When they had destroyed the Orthodox, the turn came for the Protestants. The initial situation does not last long. During that time they infiltrate the churches, putting their men in leadership. They find out the weaknesses of pastors. Some might be ambitious men; some might be entrapped with the love of money. Another might have a hidden sin somewhere, with which he may be blackmailed. They explain that they would make it known and thus put their men in leadership. Then, at a certain moment the great persecution begins. In Romania, such a clamp-down happened in one day. All the Catholic bishops went to prison, along with innumerable priests, monks, and nuns. Then many Protestant pastors of all denominations were arrested. Many died in prison.

Jesus, our Lord, told Ananias: "Meet Saul of Tarsus. He will be My underground pastor, My underground worker." That is what Paul was—a pastor of an underground church. Jesus started a crash course for this underground pastor. He started it with the words, "I will show him how many things he must suffer..."

Preparation for underground work begins by studying sufferology, martyrology. Solzhenitsyn, in his book *Gulag Archipelago,* says that police officers in the former Soviet Union had a course on arrestology—the science of how to arrest people so that nobody around shall observe. If they have created a new name, *arrestology*, let us create the name of *sufferology.*

Later, we will look at the technical side of underground work, but first of all there must be a certain spiritual preparation for it. In a free country, to be a member of a church, it is enough to believe and be baptized. In the Church underground it is not enough to be a member in it. You can be baptized and you can believe, but you will not be a member of the Underground Church unless you know how to suffer. You might have the mightiest faith in the world, but if you are not prepared to suffer, then you will be taken by the police. You will get two slaps and you will declare anything. So the *preparation* for suffering is one of the essentials in the preparation for underground work.

A Christian does not panic if he is put in prison. For the rank-and-file believer, prison is a new place to witness for Christ.

For a pastor, prison is a new parish. It is a parish with no great income but with great opportunities for work. I speak a little of this in my book *With God In Solitary Confinement*. In other books I mention Morse code, which is also part of the training for the Underground Church. You know what this is—a code by which messages are conveyed. Through this code you can preach the gospel to those who are to your right and left. The prisoners always change. Some are taken out from the cell and others are put in. God has given to many Christians who have been in prison the privilege to bring to Christ, through Morse code, men whom they have never seen. Others, after many years, meet these men whom they had brought to Christ through Morse code. I have had several parishes in common cells.

In parishes in the free world on Sunday morning, you may ring a bell. If any wish, they come to church—if not, they do not come. If a man does not like your sermons this Sunday, the next Sunday he stays away. He does not come in any case if it rains. But where you have prison as your parish, you have your parishioners with you the whole day. Free parishioners look at their watch: "Already he has preached for thirty minutes. Will he never finish?" When arrested, watches are taken away from you; you have the parishioners with you the whole week and can preach to them from morning to night! They have no choice. There have never been, in the history of the Romanian or the Russian Church, so many conversions brought about as there have been in prison. So do not fear prison. Look upon it as just a new assignment given by God. I remember that when I was arrested for the second time, my wife told me as I embraced her before going away with the policemen, "Richard, remember that it is written, 'You will be brought before rulers and kings to be a testimony unto them.'"

Men can accept this. But what about the terrible tortures that are inflicted on prisoners? What will we do about these tortures? Will we be able to bear them? If I do not bear them, I put in prison another fifty or sixty men whom I know because that is what the oppressors wish from me, to betray those around me. Hence comes the great need for preparation for suffering, which must start now. *It is too difficult* to prepare yourself for it when you are already in prison.

I remember we had a case in Romania where a pastor of twenty years had sinned with a woman. Other pastors debated this question. It was said: "His sin has not been what he has done on that evening; the circumstances were such that he could not *resist* the temptation. Rather that twenty years before, when not thus tempted, he had *not* said to himself, 'During my pastoral life different things will happen to me. Among other things it will happen that I will be tempted to sexual sin. I *will not* commit it then.'" You have to prepare yourself beforehand for *all* eventualities. We have to *prepare* for suffering.

Truth About the Truth

How much each one of us can suffer depends on how much he is bound up with a cause, how dear this cause is to him, and how much it means for him.

In this respect we have had in Communist countries very big surprises. There have been preachers and writers of Christian books who have become traitors. The composer of the best hymnal of Romania became the composer of the best Communist hymnal of Romania. Everything depends on whether we have remained in the sphere of words or if we are merged with the divine realities.

God is the Truth. The Bible is the truth about the Truth. Theology is the truth about the truth about the Truth. A good sermon is the truth about the truth about the truth, about the Truth. It is not *the* Truth. The Truth is God alone. Around this Truth there is a scaffolding of words, of theologies, and of exposition. None of these is of any help in times of suffering. It is only the Truth Himself who is of help, and we have to penetrate through sermons, through theological books, through everything that is "words" and be bound up with the reality of

God Himself.

I have told in the West how Christians were tied to crosses for four days and four nights. The crosses were put on the floor and other prisoners were tortured and made to fulfill their bodily necessities upon the faces and the bodies of the crucified ones. I have since been asked, "Which Bible verse helped and strengthened you in those circumstances?" My answer is, "*No* Bible verse was of any help." It is sheer cant and religious hypocrisy to say, "This Bible verse strengthens me, or that Bible verse helps me." Bible verses alone are not meant to help. We knew Psalm 23: "The Lord is my Shepherd; I shall not want …though I walk through the valley of the shadow of death…"

When you pass through suffering you realize that it was never meant by God that Psalm 23 should strengthen you. It is the Lord who can strengthen you, not the psalm that speaks of Him doing so. It is not enough to have the psalm. You must have the One about whom the psalm speaks. We also knew the verse, "My grace is sufficient for you" (2 Corinthians 12:9). But the verse is not sufficient. It is the grace that is sufficient and not the verse.

Pastors and zealous witnesses who are handling the Word as a calling from God are in danger of giving holy words more value than they really have. Holy words are only the means to arrive at the reality expressed by them. If you are united with the Reality, the Lord Almighty, evil loses its power over you; it cannot break the Lord Almighty. If you have only the words of the Lord Almighty, you can be very easily broken.

Spiritual Exercises

The preparation for underground work is deep spiritualization. As we peel an onion in preparation for its use, so God must "peel" from us what are mere words, sensations of our enjoyments in religion, in order to arrive at the reality of our faith. Jesus has told us that "anyone [who] desires to come after" Him will have to "take up his cross," and Jesus Himself showed how heavy this cross can be. We have to be prepared for this.

Look at the world's way! A pornographic magazine or an advertisement inflames the imagination. In just the same way, we have to inflame the imagination by having before us spiritual realities. We have to make spiritual exercises. I am very sorry that spiritual exercises are almost unknown in Protestantism. We have to revive them in the Underground Church. Spiritual exercises may have been misused by some Catholics, and then the Reformation came. There exists always the movement of the pendulum. If one has fallen to one extreme, another will fall into the other extreme.

Because some abused the use of false spiritual exercises, others would not make spiritual exercises at all. We have to have not only our moments of prayer in which we speak, but we should have moments of meditation and contemplation. We can read in Hebrews 11 the long list of those who were sawn asunder, burned on stakes, and devoured by lions, but we must also visualize these things. Now I am before lions, I am beaten, I am in danger of being burned, etc. How do I behave in this matter?

I remember my last Sunday school class before I left Romania. I took a group of ten to fifteen boys and girls on a Sunday morning, not to a church, but to the zoo. Before the cage of lions I told them, "Your forefathers in faith were thrown before such wild beasts for their faith. Know that you also will have to suffer. You will not be thrown before lions, but you will have to suffer at the hands of men who would be much worse than lions. Decide here and now whether you wish to pledge allegiance to Christ." They had tears in their eyes when they said, "Yes."

We have to make the preparation now before we are imprisoned. In prison you lose everything. You are undressed and given a prisoner's suit. No more nice furniture, nice carpets, or nice curtains. You do not have a wife anymore and you do not have your children. You do not have your library and you never see a flower. Nothing of what makes life pleasant remains. Nobody resists who has renounced the pleasures of life beforehand. There is a verse in Colossians about putting to death your members which are on earth. Ignorant and zealous Catholics have imposed some superstitions and penances. Protestants have given up mortification altogether. But there exists a Christian mortification, a "giving up" of the joys of the earth. The Christian who prepares himself for this now will not suffer the loss of them when he is in prison. You have to use the things of the world without allowing an emotional attachment.

I personally use an exercise. I live in the United States of America. Can you imagine what an American supermarket looks like? You find there many delicious things. I look at everything and say to myself, "I can go without this thing and that thing; this thing is very nice, but I can go without; this third thing I can go without, too." I visited the whole supermarket and did not spend one dollar. I had the joy of seeing many beautiful things and the second joy of knowing that I can go without.

We also had liberal modernist theologians. None of them resisted any torture. "Why should I die for a dead God and a problematic Bible? If the stories of Adam and Eve are not true, if Joshua did not stop the sun, if the prophecies were written many years *after* they were fulfilled, if Jesus was not born of a virgin and He did not rise bodily from the dead—then there are more lies in the Bible than in the Soviet newspaper *Pravda*. Why should I go to death for what is not true or at least remains problematic?"

Doubt Makes Traitors

I am Jewish. In Hebrew, the language that Jesus Himself spoke and in which the first revelation has been given, the word "doubt" does not exist. To doubt is as wrong for a man as it would be for him to walk on four legs—he is not meant to walk on four legs. A man walks erect; he is not a beast. To doubt is subhuman.

To every one of us doubts come, but do not allow doubts about essential doctrines of the Bible—such as the existence of God, the resurrection of Jesus Christ, or the existence of eternal life—to make a nest in your mind. Every theological or philosophical doubt makes you a potential traitor. You can allow yourself doubts while you have a nice study and you prepare sermons, and you eat well, or you write a book. Then you can allow yourself all kinds of daring ideas and doubts. When you are tortured, these doubts are changed into treason because you have to decide to live or die for this faith.

One of the most important things about the spiritual preparation of an underground worker is the solution of his doubts. In mathematics, if you do not find the solution you may have made a mistake somewhere, so you continue until you find out. Don't live with doubts, but seek their solution.

Test of Torture

Now to come to the very moment of torture. Torture is sometimes very painful. They use red-hot irons. Sometimes it is a simple beating. We have all been spanked as children and beating is just another spanking. A simple beating is very easy to take. Jesus has said we should come to Him like children, which is rather like candidates for spanking!

A doctor came to me and said, "What should I do? I think about throwing myself through the window. They call me again and again and wish to make me an informer on the Underground Church. They threaten me that they will beat me if I don't accept it. What should I do? It is terrible to think that they will beat me. I can't take it. I have the alternative to become an informer, or to throw myself through the window." I said, "You have another solution. Give a stick into your husband's hand and tell him to give you a good beating and you will see how you can bear it." Don't be afraid of a beating.

However, with us, Communists did not stop at beatings—they used very refined tortures. Now torture, you must know, can work both ways. It can harden you and strengthen your decision not to tell the police anything. There are thieves who resist any torture and would not betray those with whom they have cooperated in theft. The more you beat them the more obstinate they become. Or, torture can just break your will.

Now I will tell you of one very interesting case that was published by the Czech Communist Press. You will know that under Dubcek there was a period of relaxation and then they could publish certain things in Czechoslovakia. An article appeared at that time. Novotny, who was the predecessor of Dubcek and who was a Communist dictator, had arrested one of his intimate comrades, a Communist leader, a convinced atheist, and a member of the Central Committee of the Communist Party. (Not only Christians, Jews, or patriots were in prison. One Communist arrested another and tortured him just as they would do anybody else.) They arrested this Communist leader and put him in a prison cell alone. Electromagnetic rays, which disturb the mind, passed through this cell. A loudspeaker repeated day and night: "Is your name Joseph or not Joseph?" (His name was not Joseph.) "Think it over. Are you Joseph or are you not Joseph? The biggest criminal in America has been Dillinger, but you are a bigger criminal than Dillinger. What is your first name? Is it Joseph or is it not Joseph? You are a counter-revolutionist, you are a spy, but are you Joseph or not Joseph?"

They tried to drive him mad. Day and night. He felt that he would lose his mind. At a certain moment, he got an illumination. "I have now met unmitigated evil. If Communists torture a Christian, it is not absolutely evil because Communists believe that they will construct an earthly paradise. Christians hinder them, so it is right to torture Christians. But when a Communist tortures a Communist, it is torture for torture's sake. There is absolutely no justification for it. But wait a little bit. Every coin has two sides, every electric cable has two poles. If there is an unmitigated evil, against whom does this unmitigated evil fight? There must be an unmitigated good. This is God, and against Him they fight."

When he was called to the interrogator, he entered smiling into the room and told him that they could switch off the loud-speaker now because it had attained its result. "I have become a Christian." The officer asked him, "How did it happen?" He told him the whole story. The officer said, "Wait a little bit." He called a few of his comrades and said, "Please repeat the story before my comrades." He repeated the story, and the captain told the other police officer, "I told you that this method will not work. You have overdone it."

The devil is not all-mighty and all-wise like God. He makes mistakes. Evil torture is an excess that can be used very well spiritually.

Moment of Crisis

Torture has a moment of explosion, and the torturer waits for this critical moment. Learn how to conquer doubt and to think thoroughly. There is always one moment of crisis when you are ready to write or pronounce the name of your accomplice in the underground work, or to say where the secret printing shop is, or something of that kind. You have been tortured so much that nothing counts anymore; the fact that I should not have pain also does not count. Draw this last conclusion at the stage at which you have arrived and you will see that you will overcome this one moment of crisis; it gives you an intense inner joy. You feel that Christ has been with you in that decisive moment. Jailers today are now trained and refined, aware that there is a moment of crisis. If they cannot get anything from you in that moment, then they abandon torturing: they know its continuation to be useless.

I have been told since I was a very young Christian to read every day; and so I did also with my son, Mihai, since he was three or four, reading a page of the Bible and of the life of a saint or martyr. I read *Foxe's Book of Martyrs*; read it to your children. Teach them how martyrs overcame the moment of crisis.

There are a few more points in connection with torture. It is very important to understand what Jesus said: "Do not worry about tomorrow, for tomorrow will worry about its own things" (Matthew 6:34). I have had fourteen years of prison. Brother Hrapov had twenty-six, Wong Ming-Dao had twenty-eight. It seems impossible to bear long years of prison. You are not asked to bear it all at once. Do not bear even one day at a time—bear an hour at a time. One hour of pain everybody can bear. We have had a terrible toothache, a car accident—passing, perhaps, through untold anguish. You are not meant to bear pain more than this one present minute. What amplifies pain is the memory that I have been beaten and tortured so many times and that tomorrow they will take me again, and the day after tomorrow. Tomorrow I might not be alive—or they might not be alive. Tomorrow there can be an overthrow, as in Romania. Yesterday's beating has passed; tomorrow's torture has not come yet.

I am a professor in torturology. At first, torture is a terrible shock and a terrible pain. It does not continue to be so. Cardinal Mindszenty was not allowed to sleep for twenty-nine days and nights. After this he declared whatever they asked of him. Now, what happened? After a few days and nights and lack of sleep, or after a few days of intensive physical torture comes a moment when nothing counts for you anymore. You forget about your duties toward your wife and toward your children, toward your own good name and toward God. You become absolutely indifferent to everything. This is the critical moment when the need to breathe rightly is a reality. Practice breathing right.

The art of breathing means much in the Hindu and Buddhist religions in their exercise of yoga. Read now about different kinds of breathing in the Bible. Jesus "breathed" upon the apostles. It is said that Jesus breathed upon them the Holy Spirit. So there is a certain manner of breathing which conveys the Holy Spirit. In the Orthodox Church, at a baptism, the priest and the godparents breathe three times upon the child. When

Jesus breathed, He breathed the Holy Spirit. It is written in Acts 9 that Saul breathed out "threats and murder." There are murderers who breathe crime. It is written in the Book of Jeremiah of some "who neigh after other men's wives." It is the breathing of an adulterer. There is one breathing in high emotions. Try once to quarrel with somebody while breathing quietly, rhythmically and deeply. You will find you cannot quarrel.

Right breathing is one of the means of resisting torture. Betrayal means rupture with the whole Church. You are a Christian in whom God and so many men trust. You have been entrusted with the secrets of the Underground Church. To betray would be a powerful emotion. You cannot quarrel with somebody and shout at them while you breathe rhythmically and deeply. Neither can you pass through the deep emotion of betrayal if breathing so. Under torture, breathe as a traitor cannot breathe. Breathe rhythmically, quietly—very deep to the heel. The oxygenation gives a resistance to the whole body, which balances your reactions and gives you a poised attitude.

Another thing an underground worker must know, not with his head only, but in his fingertips: he should know that he belongs to the body of Christ. He belongs to a body that has been flogged for nearly 2,000 years. It has always been flogged, not only on Golgotha, but under the Roman emperors and by so many persecutions. It had been flogged under the Nazis and had been flogged in Russia for over seventy years. When converted I have *consciously* become part of a body that is a flogged body; a mocked body; a body spat upon; and one crowned with a crown of thorns, with nails driven into the hands and feet. I accept this as my possible future fate. I will never think upon Jesus Christ as only having been crucified 2,000 years ago. The sufferings of Jesus in His mystical body must become a reality for me.

Love Supreme

The Bible teaches some words very hard to take: "He who loves father or mother more than Me is not worthy of Me. And he who loves son or daughter more than Me is not worthy of Me" (Matthew 10:37). These words mean almost nothing in a free country.

You probably know from The Voice of the Martyrs literature that thousands of children had been taken away from their parents in the former Soviet Union because they were taught about Christ. You must love Christ more than your family. There you are before a court and the judge tells you that if you deny Christ you may keep your children. If not, this will be the last time you will see them. Your heart may break, but your answer should be, "I love God."

Nadia Sloboda left her house for four years of prison. Her children were taken from her, but she left her house singing. The children, for whom the police waited with a truck to take them as she left, told their singing mother, "Don't worry about us. Wherever they put us, we will not give up our faith." They did not. When Jesus was on the cross He not only suffered physically, He had His mother in front of Him, suffering. His mother had the Son suffering. They loved each other, but the glory of God was at stake and here any human sentiment must be secondary. Only if we take this attitude once and for all can we prepare for underground work.

Only Christ, the Great Sufferer, the Man of Sorrows, must live in us. There have been cases in Communist countries when Communist torturers threw away their rubber truncheons with which they beat a Christian and asked, "What is this halo that you have around your head? How is it that your face shines? I cannot beat you anymore." It is said of Stephen in the Bible that "his face shone." We have known cases of Communist torturers who told the prisoner, "Shout loudly, cry loudly as if I would beat you so that my comrades will think that I torture you. But I cannot beat you." Thus, you would shout without anything happening to you.

There are other cases when prisoners really are tortured,

sometimes to death. You have to choose between dying with Christ and for Christ or becoming a traitor. What is the worth of continuing to live when you will be ashamed to look into the mirror, knowing that the mirror will show you the face of a traitor?

To think in this manner is the first requisite for being an underground worker, especially an underground pastor—and what is even more important, an underground pastor's wife. She plays an exceptional role. She has to strengthen him; she has to give him courage to do all things. If she asks him for movies and for casual enjoyments of life, he cannot be an underground fighter. She has to push him to work and to fight and to sacrifice himself.

Learn to Be Silent

Another thing we have to learn in the Underground Church is to be silent. Pastors, by their very profession, are loquacious people, people who speak. Now a pastor is not meant to speak the whole time. Nobody can preach well unless he listens well. When I look back to my dealing with souls, I have won more souls by listening to them than by speaking to them. People have so many burdens on their heart, and there is nobody who has patience to listen to them. Even your own husband has no patience, or your wife, or your children. The latter are young and wish to go away somewhere. There is nobody to listen to you. If somebody finds a man who listens, he is won without much talk. In the Underground Church, silence is one of the first rules. Every superfluous word you speak can put somebody in prison. A friend of mine, a great Christian composer, went to prison because Christians had the habit of saying, "How beautiful is this song composed by Brother ____." They praised him, and for this he got fifteen years of prison. Sing the song, but do not mention the name of the one who has written it.

You cannot learn to be silent the very moment the country is taken over. You have to learn to be silent from the moment of your conversion. A Christian is a man who speaks little and with great weight. He thinks, if he should speak a word, whether it can harm or not. In the Underground Church every superfluous word can do harm.

Solzhenitsyn, the Nobel Prize winner, said in an interview that the one who had been his greatest persecutor, the one who denounced him, was his own former wife. It is written in the book of Ecclesiastes not to tell the secrets of your heart, even to your spouse. This is the Word of God. God knew that we would have an underground church, and He knew that at a certain moment a spouse might become angry against you over some question. The secretary to Solzhenitsyn was put under such pressure by the Communists (and she had been denounced by Solzhenitsyn's wife) that she finished by hanging herself. If Solzhenitsyn had kept silent, this would not have happened.

Another point that is very important: I thank God for the years I passed in solitary confinement. I was, for three years, thirty feet beneath the earth. I never heard a word. I never spoke a word. There were no books. The outward voices ceased. The guards had felt-soled shoes; you did not hear their approach. Then, with time, the inner voices ceased. We were drugged, we were beaten. I forgot my whole theology. I forgot the whole Bible. One day I observed that I had forgotten the "Our Father." I could not say it anymore. I knew that it began with "Our Father...," but I did not know the continuation. I just kept happy and said, "Our Father, I have forgotten the prayer, but you surely know it by heart. You hear it so many thousand times a day, so you assign an angel to say it for me, and I will just keep quiet." For a time my prayers were, "Jesus, I love You." And then after a little time again, "Jesus, I love You. Jesus, I love You." Then it became too difficult even to say this because we were doped with drugs that would destroy our minds. We were very hungry. We had one slice of bread a week. There were the beatings, and the tortures, and the lack of light, and other things. It became *impossible* to concentrate my mind to even say so much as, "Jesus, I love You." I abandoned it because I knew that it was necessary. The highest form of prayer I know is the quiet beating of a heart that loves Him. Jesus should just hear "tick-a-tock, tick-a-tock," and He would know that every heartbeat is for Him.

When I came out from solitary confinement and was with other prisoners and heard them speaking, I wondered why they spoke! So much of our speech is useless. Today men become acquainted with each other and one will say, "How do you do?" and the other answers, "How do you do?" What is the use of this? Then one will say, "Don't you think that the weather is fine?" and the other thinks, and says, "Yes, I think it is fine." Why do we have to speak on whether the weather is fine? We do not take earnestly the word of Jesus who says that men will be judged not for every bad word, but for every useless one. So it is written in the Bible. Useless talking in some countries means prison and death for your brother. A word of praise about your brother, if it is not necessary, may mean catastrophe. For example, somebody comes to visit you and you say "Oh! I'm sorry you were not here before—Brother W. has just left." The visitor could be an informer of the secret police. Now she will know that Brother W. is in town! Keep your mouth shut. Learn to do this now.

Permissible Stratagems

You cannot do underground work without using stratagems. I know of one case that happened in Russia. The Communists suspected that the Christians were gathering somewhere and they surveyed a street. They knew that the meeting must be there somewhere. They saw a young boy going toward the house where they supposed the meeting would be. The police stopped the boy and asked him, "Where are you going?" With a sad face, he said, "My oldest brother died, and now we gather the whole family to read his testament." The police officer was so impressed that he patted the boy and said, "Just go." The boy had not told a lie.

A brother had been taken to the police and was asked, "Do you still gather at meetings?" He answered, "Comrade captain, prayer meetings are forbidden now." To this the captain replied, "Well, it is good that you conform with this. Just go." The brother had not said that he conformed; he had not said that he did not go to meetings.

A courier of The Voice of the Martyrs went to a Communist country. He was stopped at the border and was asked, "What books do you have with you?" He said, "I have the words of Shakespeare and the words of Jehovah." The police officer did not wish to show that he was ignorant. Jehovah might be some other great British poet and to say he had not heard of Jehovah would put him to shame. He said, "Okay, okay, just pass through." These are permissible stratagems.

If angels exist as fairy tales to be told to children, I do not need them. Angels are a reality; we each have a guardian angel. Where Christians gather there are always devils, also. We have to rely on angels and upon the Holy Spirit. We are not obliged to tell an atheist tyrant the truth. We are not obliged to tell him what we are doing. It is indecent for his side to ask me questions, an impertinence.

If I would simply put to you the question, "How much money do you have in the bank?" or, "How much do you earn a month?" would it not be impertinent? Such questions should not be asked. You are not meant to ask a girl, "Do you have a boyfriend, or not? Are you already in love with somebody?" She might not wish to tell you something like this. So a man is not meant to press me about my religious activity if I do not wish to tell it to him. It is mixing in my private affairs. The atheistic state has no right to ask such questions, and we are not meant to answer them.

At interrogation, they put to you all kinds of questions. The Communists told me: "You are a Christian and you are a pastor. You are meant to speak the truth. Now tell us, who are the leaders of the Underground Church? Where do you gather? Who do you meet? Who are the leaders in the different towns?" If I had revealed the truth, there would have been innumerable arrests of men who, in their turn, would have declared the truth, etc. This must be resisted. Where the results of resisting are beatings and tortures, you have to take them upon yourself, even if you die.

I know a pastor who today has pains as great as I had when I was beaten, because he played rugby. Something happened to his foot and it gives him terrible pains. For rugby, I can take upon myself pains and, when the pain disappears, will again play rugby knowing that some other accident might happen. So we take upon ourselves physical pains for rugby, which is a sport, a pleasure, and healthy for the body. In the same way, you take the physical pains of torture upon yourself to protect your brethren from being arrested. The worst thing that might happen because of this is that you will die under tortures. But to die is the most natural thing in the world.

A beggar stopped at the house of a rich man and said, "Could I please sleep one night here? I do not have a place to sleep." The rich man said, "Go away from here, beggar. This is not a hotel." The poor man said, "I apologize; I will go further." Then he said, "But would you first please answer me a question? I looked to this house. I found it so beautiful. Who has made this house?" Now the rich man felt flattered somehow and said, "This is the house built by my grandfather." "And where is your grandfather now?" "He died a long time ago." "Who lived in the house after your grandfather?" "Well, my father." "Is he still alive?" "No, he also died." "And who lives in the house now?" "I." "And will you also die?" "Yes." "And who will live in the house after you die?" "Well, I hope my children." Then the beggar said, "Why do you shout at me? You said that this is not a hotel. It *is* a hotel room. You pack your things, somebody else comes." Your mortality is obvious; take it as your view of life in general. If God wishes me to die today, He does not need a torturer. I can die by a heart attack without a torturer. So the torturer can never shorten my life by even one day. Never can the best restaurant with the finest dainties prolong my life one day. I die when I am called by God.

Treacherous Quarreling

Not the slightest quarrel is permitted in the Underground Church. Every quarrel in the Underground Church means arrests, beatings, and perhaps death. Our adversaries watch and listen. They have their informers in the Underground Church. Whenever there is a quarrel, there are reciprocal accusations. The one would say to the other, "When you were with Brother Smith, you did this, etc." So the police get Smith.

Quarrels always bring up names and bring out facts. Therefore, the word is written in the Bible, "A servant of the Lord must not quarrel but be gentle to all" (2 Timothy 2:24). I know of one town in Romania where there was a terrible quarrel between two congregations. The one was Baptist and the other was Exclusive Brethren. It was such a terrible quarrel that it resulted in the arrest of the leaders of both congregations.

It would be better to start today to be a saint. It will be too late to start to be holy when you go to heaven! You will not know how to start it. You have to start it now. Then, if in the case of a takeover it would be better not to quarrel, the best thing is not to quarrel now.

Sadly there are quarrels among organizations that work in dangerous circumstances. As far as possible they should be avoided. Even a family quarrel can mean death. I was in the same prison cell with a man who had a girlfriend. As it happens at a young age, he met another girl whom he preferred to the first girl. But to that girl he had told different secrets, and the girl informed the Secret Police. He got life-long prison. He went mad in jail.

The preparation for underground work is basic to the preparation for a normal Christian worker, only it is much deeper and it has to become much more real—a part of life. I know countries where many congregations are destroyed by a quarrel between two pastors or two elders of the church. It happens everywhere, but in an oppressive country it means imprisonment and perhaps death.

Resisting Brainwashing

One of the greatest methods is not only physical torture, it is brainwashing. We have to know how to resist brainwashing. Brainwashing exists in the free world, too. The press, radio, and television brainwash us. There exists no motive in the world to drink Coca-Cola. You drink it because you are brainwashed. Plain water is surely better than Coca-Cola. But nobody advertises, "Drink water, drink water." If water were advertised, we would drink water.

Some have driven this technique of brainwashing to its extreme. The methods vary, but brainwashing in my Romanian prison consisted essentially of this: we had to sit seventeen hours on a form that gave no possibility to lean, and we were not allowed to close our eyes. For seventeen hours a day we had to hear, "Communism is good, Communism is good, Communism is good,…; Christianity is dead, Christianity is dead, Christianity is dead,…; Give up, give up,…" You were bored after one minute of this but you had to hear it the whole seventeen hours for weeks, months, years even, without any interruption. I can assure you, it is not easy. It is one of the worst tortures, much worse than physical torture. But Christ has foreseen all things because with Him there is no time. Future, past, present are one and the same: He knows all things from the beginning. Communists invented brainwashing too late! Christ had already invented the opposite of brainwashing—heartwashing. He has said, "Blessed are the pure in heart, for they shall see God" (Matthew 5:8).

Stephen, the first martyr for Christ, had around him hundreds with big stones in their hands to throw at him. He said,

"I see…" And the wife of Stephen probably thought he saw the danger he was in and would run away. But he said, "I see *Jesus* standing at the right hand of God." Perhaps she said (it is not recorded), "Don't you see all the mob around you ready to throw stones at you?" "Oh yes! I see some little ants there below not worth mentioning. I look to *Jesus*." He did not look to those who wished to kill him. Blessed are the pure in heart.

I had passed through brainwashing for over two years. The Communists would have said that my brain was still dirty. In the same rhythm in which they said, "Christianity is dead," I and others repeated to ourselves, "Christ also has been dead, Christ also has been dead." But we knew He rose from the dead. We remembered that we lived in the communion of saints.

We usually believe that the saints who have passed to the Lord are somewhere in the skies about the stars. The Bible tells us where they are. "Since we are surrounded by so great a cloud of witnesses…" (Hebrews 12:1). Why should they sit among the stars? They are here where the real fighters and sufferers are. In the world of the Spirit there exists no here and there. The notions of space and time do not exist in the world of the Spirit. We were isolated in prison, but they were around us. We felt the presence of the saints of all times. I personally had very much the feeling of the presence of Mary Magdalene. I thought during the brainwashing, "What are they telling me, that Christianity is dead? Supposing they are right, what difference does it make? Supposing there is not one single Christian in the world except me, what difference would it make? Mary Magdalene just loved Jesus. If Jesus was dead, she loved a dead Jesus. She stayed near the tomb of the dead Jesus who could do nothing for her. He could not lift a finger for her; He could do no miracle for her; He could not speak to her a word of comfort. He could not wipe away a tear—nothing. He was the Savior. So, what if you tell me He is dead? I love Him just as much as if He would be alive. If the whole Church had died or lost its faith, it is no motive for me to lose my faith."

We have to arrive at a certitude of faith. I have told you that the words "to doubt" do not exist in Hebrew. This phrase does not exist in the Old Testament. May I point out to you another word that does not exist in Hebrew? I was often accused by leaders of the World Council of Churches. They wrote against me: "Wurmbrand paints the situation behind the Iron Curtain in white and black. It is not so. There exists the gray." I reply that I accept this if they show me from the whole of the New Testament the word "gray." There exists in the New Testament many colors—"gray," a mixture, does not exist. A thing is true or untrue; it is right or it is wrong. It is white or it is black. You have to go with the world or you have to go with Christ. So the Old Testament, the Hebrew, does not have the words "to doubt." We must be sure in these problems of faith as we are sure about the table of addition or multiplication. Two and two are four. This is true. If my family is alive or has been killed, if I have enough or if I starve, if I am free or if I am in prison, if I am beaten or if I am caressed, the truth of mathematics does not change. Two plus two caresses are four caresses, and two plus two beatings make four beatings.

The certainty of Truth and a love like that of Mary Magdalene enable you to resist brainwashing. Resist to the extreme.

I do not wish to pose as a hero. I am a man, and as every man, I have my flaws and my weaknesses. Therefore, we exist as a Church to encourage each other in moments of weakness. Under such terrible pressure I, at a certain moment, whispered to a brother near me—a Presbyterian minister and a very good Christian—"Brother, I believe that I have lost my faith. I don't think I am anymore a believer." He, with a smile that never left him, asked me, "But did you ever believe?" I said, "Yes, surely I did." He said, "Then remember one verse of the Bible. When the virgin Mary came to Elizabeth, Elizabeth told her, 'Blessed is she who *believed*.' It is the past tense. If you have *believed* in the past, you are blessed. Live on this blessedness." I cannot tell you what those words meant to me under those circumstances.

I do not know how sound the theology is, but we did not live on theology at that time. We lived on past memories. Therefore, the Bible teaches us that we should bless the Lord and not forget His past blessings. Remember the past blessings even if you pass through a dark night of the soul.

Overcoming Solitude

One of the greatest problems for an underground fighter is to know how to fill up his solitude. We had absolutely no books. Not only no Bible, but no books, no scrap of paper, and no pencil. We never heard a noise, and there was absolutely nothing to distract our attention. We looked at the walls, that was all. Now normally a mind under such circumstances becomes mad. Read great books about prison life (*Papillon* and other such books that are very valuable to read for a future underground worker) just to catch the atmosphere of prison as much as a free man can catch it. You will see the maddening influence of being alone for years with nothing to distract the mind. I can tell you from my own experience how I avoided becoming mad, but this again has to be prepared by a life of spiritual exercise beforehand. How much can you be alone without the Bible? How much can you bear to be with yourself without switching on the radio, or a record player, etc.?

I, and many other prisoners, did it like this. We never slept during the night. We slept during the day. The whole night we were awake. You know that a psalm says, "Behold, bless the Lord, all you servants of the Lord, who by night stand in the house of the Lord" (Psalm 134:1). One prayer at night is worth ten prayers during the day.

All great sins and crimes are committed during the night. The great robberies, drunkenness, reveling, adultery—this whole life of sin is a night life. During the day everyone has to work in a factory, college, or somewhere. The demonic forces are forces of the night, and therefore, it is so important to oppose them during the night. Vigils are very important. In the free world, vigils are largely unknown. In my country, even before the Communist takeover, we had vigils. My son, Mihai, when he was three or four years of age, knew of vigils. The whole night we would pass in prayer. Small children of three and four, while we would pray, would also pray a little, then they would kick each other. We would scold them a bit, then they would pray again a little, and then they would fall asleep under some tables. That is how they were brought up with vigils.

In solitary confinement we awoke when the other prisoners went to bed. We filled our time with a program that was so heavy we could not fulfill it. We started with a prayer, a prayer in which we traveled through the whole world. We prayed for each country, for where we knew the names of towns and men, and we prayed for great preachers. It took a good hour or two to come back. We prayed for pilots, and for those on the sea, and for those who were in prisons. The Bible tells us about one of the great joys we can have, even in a prison cell: "Rejoice with those who rejoice" (Romans 12:15). I rejoiced that there were families somewhere who gathered with their children, read the Bible together, told jokes, and were so happy with each other. Somewhere there was a boy who loved a young girl and dated her; I could be happy about them. There they had a prayer meeting; and there was someone who studied; and there is somebody who enjoyed good food, etc. We could rejoice with those who rejoiced.

After having traveled through the whole world, I read the Bible from memory. To memorize the Bible is very important for an underground worker.

Just to make us laugh also a little bit, I will tell you one thing that happened. Once while I lay on the few planks that were my bed, I read from memory the Sermon on the Mount, according to Luke. I arrived at the part where it is said, "When you are persecuted…for the Son of Man's sake, rejoice in that day and leap for joy" (Luke 6:22,23a). I remembered it written like this. I said, "How could I commit such a sin of neglect?

Christ has said that we have to do two different things. One, to rejoice, I have done. The second, to 'leap for joy,' I have not done." So I jumped. I came down from my bed and I began to jump around. In prison, the door of a cell has a peep hole through which the warden looks into the cell. He happened to look in while I jumped around. So he believed that I had become mad. They had an order to behave very well with madmen so that their shouting and banging on the wall should not disturb the order of the prison. The guard immediately entered, quieted me down and said, "You will be released; you can see everything will be all right. Just remain quiet. I will bring you something." He brought me a big loaf of bread. Our portion was one slice of bread a week, and now I had a whole loaf, *plus cheese*. It was white. Never just eat cheese; first of all admire its whiteness. It is beautiful to look upon. He also brought me sugar. He spoke a few nice words again and locked the door and left.

I said, "I will eat these things after having finished my chapter from St. Luke." I lay down again and tried to remember where I had left off. "Yes, at 'when you are persecuted for My name's sake, rejoice'...and leap for joy because great is your reward." I looked at the loaf of bread and the cheese. Really, the reward *was* great!

So the next task is to think of the Bible and to meditate upon it. Every night, I composed a sermon beginning with "Dear brethren and sisters" and finishing with "Amen." After I composed it, I delivered it. I put them afterwards in very short rhymes so that I could remember them. My books *With God In Solitary Confinement* and *If Prison Walls Could Speak* contain some of these sermons. I have memorized three hundred and fifty of them. When I came out of prison, I wrote some of them down. Some fifty of them have been published in these two books. They were sermons I just uttered to God and to the angels. Angels have wings, and they take the thoughts to somebody else. (Now these sermons are published in many languages and are used.) We filled our time like this. I composed books and poems. I thought about my wife and children. Every night I told myself jokes, but always new jokes that I had not known before so that they were all optimistic. They showed how I felt then. One of the jokes was: A woman said to her husband, "Peter, what should I do? I sat on my false teeth, and I broke them." The husband said, "Be happy, imagine how it would be if you had sat on your natural teeth." So I saw the good side of things.

Out of bread I made chessmen, some of them whitened with a little bit of chalk and the others gray. I played chess with myself. Never believe that Bob Fisher is the greatest chess master of the world. He won the last match with Spassky. He won eight games and lost two. I, in three years, never lost a game; I always won either with white or gray!

I have told you all these things because they belong to the secrets of the underground worker when he suffers. Never allow your mind to become distressed because then the Communists have you entirely in their hands. Your mind must be continually exercised. It must be alert, it must think. It must, everyone according to his abilities, compose different things, etc.

True Identity

The Underground Church is not something new. After having worked in the Church underground I read the New Testament with new eyes. I read in the Acts of the apostles examples where apostles and disciples bore "other" names than formerly, and there are many examples of this throughout the New Testament (Revelation 2:17 being a sublime example).

- "JOSEPH, called BARSABUS, who was surnamed JUSTUS" (Acts 1:23).
- "JOSES, who was also named BARNABAS by the apostles" (Acts 4:36).
- "SIMEON who was called NIGER" (Acts 13:1).
- "JUDAS who was also named BARSABAS" (Acts 15:22).

- "JESUS who is called JUSTUS" (Colossians 4:11).

Why should James and John be termed "sons of thunder" and a Simon be called "Peter?" I had never known an explanation of this. We find so many names changed in the New Testament. Now that is exactly what happens in the Church underground. I had many names. When I went into a town or village, they would never say that Brother Wurmbrand had come. In one town it was Vasile, in another it was Georghescu, in another it was Ruben, etc. When I was arrested, I was Richard Wurmbrand, called so-and-so.

I believe in the literal inspiration of the Bible, not only in the verbal inspiration. Why then does it contain seemingly "useless" words? It was written in Luke, "Jesus prayed in a certain place." You have to be somewhere when you pray. Then why these words, "in a certain place?" It is written, "He came to a certain city." Every city is a certain city, but this is exactly the language of the Underground Church. When I came back from a journey I would tell my wife, "I was in a certain city and a certain place where I met a certain brother. We decided that at a certain hour we would meet in a certain house."

Jesus wished to have supper with His disciples (Luke 22:7–13). Now, the normal thing for Him would have been to say, "Go on to that-and-that street at number so-and-so, ask about Mr. XYZ, and there prepare a supper." Instead of this He says, "When you are entered into the city, there shall a man meet you, bearing a pitcher of water; follow him into the house where he entereth in." (It would be a rare thing at that time for a man to "bear a pitcher of water" since women were those who went to the well.) This is exactly how we do it; when we have a prayer meeting we do not give an address because we do not know who is the informer. We say, "Stand at the corner of 'that' street, or sit there in a public park and you will see passing a man with a blue necktie or other sign. Go after him." If anybody asks the other, "What is your name?" then we know he is an informer of the Secret Police.

The Underground Church is something that existed already in the time of the writing of the New Testament. We have critics who say that what we do is unlawful before God because a Church should not work underground. We have to obey the authorities. The World Council of Churches accuse us, but they give money to guerrillas who do not obey the authorities. In the Bible it is written that he who has authority is a ruler who punishes evil and rewards good. An authority that forbids the Word of God puts itself outside of any human sphere. No Bible verse applies to it. Every authority has its laws and has its injustices and abuses because no government consists of saints. It consists of sinners. Every authority does right and wrong things. The principal thing is that they should not hinder a caterpillar from becoming a butterfly. They should not hinder a bud from becoming a flower; they should not hinder a sinner from becoming a saint. As long as they allow me this, I do not expect from them to be saints dropped from heaven. I expect from them that they do some good things and should sometimes have wrong laws which they can change after two or three years. I will respect them as an authority. But if they take away the very sense of my life, which is to prepare myself for a more beautiful existence in heaven, I do not feel any duty toward this authority. Our Mission just continues its underground work to help the Underground Church in Communist and Muslim countries.

I have given you just a glimpse of the problems which this Underground Church has so that you might, somehow, have an image of what it looks like.

May God bless you.

Also by Richard Wurmbrand:
Tortured for Christ
From Suffering to Triumph
In the Face of Surrender
In God's Underground
If Prison Walls Could Speak
With God in Solitary Confinement
Christ on the Jewish Road
The Answer to the Atheist's Handbook
Marx & Satan
Alone With God
Reaching Toward the Heights

Suffering: *the* Sacrifice *of* Christian Hedonism

John Piper

Excerpted from *Desiring God*, © 1996 by John Piper
(Sisters, Oregon: Multnomah Books).
Used by permission of Multnomah Publishers, Inc.
For requested use only, not to be copied for any other purposes.

Sitting at the Feet of a Suffering Saint

I have never been the same since sitting at the feet of Richard Wurmbrand. It was literally at his feet. He took off his shoes and sat in a chair on the slightly raised platform at Grace Baptist Church in south Minneapolis. (I learned later it had to do with damage to his feet during the torture that he had received in a Romanian prison.) Before him—and below him—sat about a dozen pastors. He spoke of suffering. Again and again he said that Jesus "chose" suffering. He "chose" it. It did not merely happen to him. He "chose" it. "No one takes my life from me. I lay it down of my own will" (John 10:18). He asked us if we would choose suffering for the sake of Christ.

Wurmbrand's devotional book, *Reaching Toward the Heights*, introduces him like this: Richard Wurmbrand is an evangelical Lutheran pastor of Jewish origin who was born in 1909 in Romania. When the Communists seized his native land in 1945, he became a leader in the underground church. In 1948 he and his wife, Sabina, were arrested, and he served fourteen years in Red Prisons, including three years in solitary confinement in a subterranean cell, never seeing the sun, the stars, or flowers. He saw no one except his guards and torturers. Christian friends in Norway purchased his freedom for $10,000 in 1964.[1]

How Beautiful Is Sacrifice?

One of the stories he tells is about a Cistercian abbot who was interviewed on Italian television. The interviewer was especially interested in the Cistercian tradition of living in silence and solitude. So he asked the abbot, "And what if you were to realize at the end of your life that atheism is true, that there is no God? Tell me, what if it were true?"

The abbot replied, "Holiness, silence, and sacrifice are beautiful in themselves, even without promise of reward. I still will have used my life well."

Few glimpses into the meaning of life have had a greater impact on my contemplations about suffering. The first impact of the abbot's response was a superficial, romantic surge of glory. But then something stuck. It did not sit well. Something was wrong. At first I could not figure it out. Then I turned to the great Christian sufferer, the apostle Paul, and was stunned by the gulf between him and the abbot.

Paul's answer to the interviewer's question was utterly contrary to the abbot's answer. The interviewer had asked, "What if your way of life turns out to be based on a falsehood, and there is no God?" The abbot's answer in essence was, "It was a good and noble life anyway." Paul gave his answer in 1 Corinthians 15:19, "If for this life only we have hoped in Christ, we are of all men most to be pitied." This is the exact opposite of the abbot's answer.

Why did Paul not agree with the monk? Why didn't Paul say, "Even if Christ is not raised from the dead, and even if there is no God, a life of love and labor and sacrifice and suffering is a good life"? Why didn't he say that "even without the reward of resurrection, we are not to be pitied"? Why did he say instead, "If our hope in Christ proves false in the end, we are to be pitied more than anyone"?

Does Life Go Better with Christ?

This is an utterly crucial question for the Christian Church, especially in prosperous, comfortable lands like America and Western Europe. How many times do we hear Christian testimonies to the effect that becoming a Christian has made life easier? I recently heard the quarterback of a professional football team say that after he prayed to receive Christ, he felt good about the game again and was proud of their 8 and 8 record because he was able to go out every Sunday and give it his best.

It seems that most Christians in the prosperous West describe the benefits of Christianity in terms that would make it a good life, even if there were no God and no resurrection. Think of all the psychological benefits and relational benefits. And of course these are true and biblical: the fruit of the Holy Spirit is love, joy, and peace. So if we get love, joy, and peace from believing these things, then is it not a good life to live, even if it turns out to be based on a falsehood? Why should we be pitied?

What's wrong with Paul, then? Was he not living the abundant life? Why would he say that, if there is no resurrection, we are of all men most to be pitied? It does not seem to be pitiable to live your three score and ten in a joyful and satisfying delusion, if that delusion makes no difference whatever for the future. If delusion can turn emptiness and meaninglessness into happiness, then why not be deluded?

The answer seems to be that the Christian life for Paul was not the so-called good life of prosperity and ease. Instead it was a life of freely chosen suffering beyond anything we ordinarily experience. Paul's belief in God, and his confidence in resurrection, and his hope in eternal fellowship with Christ, did not produce a life of comfort and ease that would have been satisfying even without resurrection. No, what his hope produced was a life of chosen suffering. Yes, he knew joy unspeakable. But it was a "rejoicing in hope" (Romans 12:12). And that hope freed him to embrace sufferings that he never would have chosen apart from the hope of his own resurrection and the resurrection of those for whom he suffered. If there is no resurrection, Paul's sacrificial choices, by his own testimony, were pitiable.

Yes, there was joy and a sense of great significance in his suffering. But the joy was there only because of the joyful hope beyond suffering. This is the point of Romans 5:3,4. "We exult in our afflictions, knowing that affliction produces endurance, and endurance produces proven genuineness, and genuineness produces *hope*." So there is joy in affliction. But the joy comes because of the hope that affliction itself is helping to secure and increase. So if there is no hope, Paul is a fool to embrace this affliction, and even more foolish to rejoice in it. But there is hope. And so Paul chooses a way of life that would be foolish and pitiable without the hope of joy beyond the grave. He answers Richard Wurmbrand's question, Yes. He chooses suffering.

Is There a Difference between Conflict and Cancer?

Let's take a brief detour for a moment. Someone may ask at this point, "What about suffering I do not choose? Like cancer. Or the death of my child in a car accident? Or a severe depression? Is this chapter about any of that?" My answer is that most of this chapter is about the suffering Christians accept as part of a choice to be openly Christian in risky situations. And all situations are risky, one way or the other.

The most significant difference between sickness and persecution is that persecution is an intentional hostility from someone because we are known to be Christians, but sickness is not. Therefore, in some situations, to choose to be public Christians is to choose a way of life that accepts suffering, if God wills (1 Peter 4:19). But suffering may result from living as a Christian even when there is no intentional hostility from unbelievers. For example, a Christian may go to a disease-ridden village to minister, and contract the disease. This is suffering as a Christian, but it is not "persecution." It is a choice to suffer, if God wills, but not from the hostility of others.

But then, when you stop to think about it, all of life, if it is lived earnestly by faith in the pursuit of God's glory and the salvation of others, is like the Christian who goes to the disease-ridden village. The suffering that comes is part of the price of living where you are in obedience to the call of God. In choosing to follow Christ in the way he directs, we choose all that this path includes under his sovereign providence. Thus all suffering that comes in the path of obedience is suffering with Christ and for Christ—whether it is cancer or conflict. And it is "chosen"—that is, we willingly take the path of obedience where the suffering befalls us, and we do not murmur against God. We may pray—as Paul did—that the suffering be removed (2 Corinthians 12:8); but if God wills, we embrace it in the end, as part of the cost of discipleship in the path of obedience on the way to heaven.

All Suffering in a Christian Calling Is with Christ and for Christ

All experiences of suffering in the path of Christian obedience, whether from persecution or sickness or accident, have this in common: they all threaten our faith in the goodness of God and tempt us to leave the path of obedience. Therefore, every triumph of faith and all perseverance in obedience are testimonies to the goodness of God and the preciousness of Christ— whether the enemy is sickness, Satan, sin, or sabotage.

Therefore all suffering, of every kind, that we endure in the path of our Christian calling is a suffering "with Christ" and "for Christ." *With* him in the sense that the suffering comes to us as we are walking with him by faith, and in the sense that it is endured in the strength that he supplies through his sympathizing high-priestly ministry (Hebrews 4:15). *For* him in the sense that the suffering tests and proves our allegiance to his goodness and power, and in the sense that it reveals his worth as an all-sufficient compensation and prize.

Satan's and God's Design in the Same Suffering

Not only that, the suffering of sickness and the suffering of persecution have this in common: they are both intended by Satan for the destruction of our faith, and governed by God for the purifying of our faith.

Take first the case of persecution. In 1 Thessalonians 3:4,5 Paul describes his concern for the faith of the Thessalonians in the face of persecution:

> When we were with you, we told you in advance that we were going to suffer affliction; and so it happened, as you know. On account of this, when I could endure it no longer, I also sent to find out about your faith, lest somehow the tempter might have tempted you, and our labor should be in vain.

What is plain here is that the design of the "tempter" in this affliction is to destroy faith.

But Satan is not the only designer in this affair. God rules over Satan and gives him no more leash than can accomplish his ultimate purposes. Those purposes are the opposite of Satan's, even in the very same experience of suffering. For example, the writer of Hebrews 12 shows his readers how not to lose heart in persecution, because of God's loving purposes in it.

> Consider [Christ] who has endured such hostility by sinners against himself, so that you may not grow weary and lose heart. You have not yet resisted to the point of shedding blood in your striving against sin; and you have forgotten the exhortation which is addressed to you as sons, "My son, do not regard lightly the discipline of the Lord, nor faint when you are reproved by him; for those whom the Lord loves he disciplines, and he scourges every son whom he receives" [Proverbs 3:11,12]. It is for discipline that you endure...All discipline for the moment seems not to be joyful, but sorrowful; yet to those who have been trained by it, afterwards it yields the peaceful fruit of righteousness.

Here is suffering that is coming from "hostility by sinners." This means that Satan has a hand in it, just as he did in the suffering of Jesus (Luke 22:3). Nevertheless, this very suffering is described as governed by God in such a way that it has the loving and fatherly design of purifying discipline. So Satan has one design for our suffering in persecution and God has a different design for that very same experience.

But persecution is not unique in this. The same is true of sickness. Both the design of Satan and the design of God are evident in 2 Corinthians 12:7–10.

> There was given me a thorn in the flesh, a messenger of Satan to buffet me—to keep me from exalting myself! Concerning this I entreated the Lord three times that it might depart from me. And He has said to me, "My grace is sufficient for you, for power is perfected in weakness." Most gladly, therefore, I will rather boast about my weaknesses, that the power of Christ may dwell in me. There-

fore I am well content with weaknesses, with insults, with distresses, with persecutions, with difficulties, for Christ's sake; for when I am weak, then I am strong.

Here Paul's physical suffering—the thorn in the flesh—is called "a messenger of Satan." But the design of this suffering is "to keep [Paul] from exalting [himself]," which never would have been Satan's design. So the point is that Christ sovereignly accomplishes his loving, purifying purpose, by overruling Satan's destructive attempts. Satan is always aiming to destroy our faith; but Christ magnifies his power in weakness.

Are Suffering from Persecution and Sickness Distinguishable?

Another reason for not distinguishing sharply between persecution and sickness is that the pain from persecution and the pain from sickness are not always distinguishable. Decades after his torture for Christ in a Romanian prison, Richard Wurmbrand still suffered from the physical effects. Was he being "persecuted" as he endured the pain in his feet thirty years later? Or consider the apostle Paul. Among the sufferings that he listed as a "servant of Christ" was the fact that he was shipwrecked three times and spent a night and a day in the water. He also says his sufferings for Christ included "labor and hardship, through many sleepless nights, in hunger and thirst, often without food, in cold and exposure" (2 Corinthians 11:25,27).

Suppose that he got pneumonia from all this work and exposure. Would that pneumonia have been "persecution"? Paul did not make a distinction between being beaten by rods, or having a boating accident, or being cold while traveling between towns. For him any suffering that befell him while serving Christ was part of the "cost" of discipleship. When a missionary's child gets diarrhea, we think of this as part of the price of faithfulness. But if any parent is walking in the path of obedience to God's calling, it is the same price. What turns sufferings into sufferings "with" and "for" Christ is not how intentional our enemies are, but how faithful we are. If we are Christ's, then what befalls us is for his glory and for our good whether it is caused by enzymes or by enemies.

Is Gluttony the Alternative to Resurrection?

Now we turn from our brief detour to Paul's amazing statement in 1 Corinthians 15:19 that the life he has chosen is pitiable if there is no resurrection. In other words Christianity, as Paul understands it, is not the best way to maximize pleasure, if this life is all that there is. Paul tells us the best way to maximize our pleasures in this life. "If the dead are not raised, let us eat and drink, for tomorrow we die" (1 Corinthians 15:32). He does not mean something so naive as sheer epicureanism and debauchery. That is not the best way to maximize your pleasures, as anyone knows who has followed the path of alcoholism and gluttony. Drunks and gluttons are to be pitied just like Christians, if there is no resurrection.

But what he does mean by the phrase, "Let us eat and drink," is that, without the hope of resurrection, one should pursue ordinary pleasures and avoid extraordinary suffering. This is the life Paul has rejected as a Christian. Thus, if the dead are not raised, and if there is no God and no heaven, he would not have pummeled his body the way he did. He would not have turned down wages for his tentmaking the way he did. He would not have walked into five whippings of thirty-nine lashes. He would not have endured three beatings with rods. He would not have risked his life from robbers and deserts and rivers and cities and seas and angry mobs. He would not have accepted sleepless nights and cold and exposure. He would not have endured so long with backsliding and hypocritical Christians (2 Corinthians 11:23–29). Instead he would have simply lived the good life of comfort and ease as a respectable Jew with the prerogatives of Roman citizenship.

When Paul says, "If the dead are not raised, let us eat and drink," he does not mean, "Let's all become lechers." He means, there is a normal, simple, comfortable, ordinary life of human delights that we may enjoy with no troubling thoughts of heaven or hell or sin or holiness or God—*if* there is no resurrection from the dead. And what stunned me about this train of thought is that many professing Christians seem to aim at just this, and call it Christianity.

Paul did not see his relation to Christ as the key to maximizing his physical comforts and pleasures *in this life*. No, Paul's relation to Christ was a call to choose suffering—a suffering that was beyond what would make atheism "meaningful" or "beautiful" or "heroic." It was a suffering that would have been utterly foolish and pitiable to choose if there is no resurrection into the joyful presence of Christ.

An Almost Unbelievable Indictment of Western Christianity

This was the astonishing thing I finally saw in pondering Wurmbrand's story about the Cistercian abbot. In Paul's radically different viewpoint I saw an almost unbelievable indictment of Western Christianity. Am I overstating this? Judge for yourself. How many Christians do you know who could say, "The lifestyle I have chosen as a Christian would be utterly foolish and pitiable if there is no resurrection"? How many Christians are there who could say, "The suffering I have freely chosen to embrace for the cause of Christ would be a pitiable life if there is no resurrection"? As I see it, these are shocking questions.

Christianity: A Life of Chosen Suffering

"If we have hoped in Christ in this life only, we are of all men most to be pitied" (1 Corinthians 15:19). The Christian life for Paul was a life of chosen sacrifice on earth, that we might gain the joy of fellowship with Christ in the age to come. Here is how he put it:

> Whatever things were gain to me, these things I have counted as loss for the sake of Christ. More than that, I

count all things to be loss on account of the surpassing value of knowing Christ Jesus my Lord, for whom I have suffered the loss of all things, and count them but rubbish in order that I may gain Christ...I share his sufferings ...that if possible I may attain the resurrection from the dead (Philippians 3:7–11).

I say it again: the call of Christ is a call to live a life of sacrifice and loss and suffering that would be foolish to live, if there were no resurrection from the dead. This is a conscious choice for Paul. Listen to his protest: "If the dead are not raised...why am I in peril every hour? I protest, brothers, by my exultation in you which I have in Christ Jesus our Lord, I die every day!" (1 Corinthians 15:29–31). This is what Paul has chosen. He "protests" because he does not *have* to live this way. He chooses it: "In peril every hour!" "Dying every day!" This is why he says he should be pitied if there is no resurrection from the dead. He chooses a path that leads to trouble and pain virtually every day of his life. "I die every day."

Why? Why Does He Do It?

This is not normal. Human beings flee suffering. We move to safer neighborhoods. We choose milder climates. We buy air conditioners. We take aspirin. We come in out of the rain. We avoid dark streets. We purify our water. We do not normally choose a way of life that would put us in "peril every hour." Paul's life is out of sync with ordinary human choices. Virtually no advertising slogans lure us into daily dying.

So what is driving the apostle Paul to "share abundantly in Christ's sufferings" (2 Corinthians 1:5) and to be a "fool for Christ's sake" (1 Corinthians 4:10)? Why would he make choices that expose him to being "hungry and thirsty...poorly clothed ...roughly treated...homeless...reviled...persecuted...slandered...as the scum of the world, the dregs of all things" (1 Corinthians 4:11–13)?

"I Will Show Him How Much He Must Suffer"

Perhaps it was simple obedience to Christ's commission expressed in Acts 9:15,16. When Jesus sent Ananias to open Paul's eyes after he was blinded on the road to Damascus, he said, "Go, for [Paul] is a chosen instrument of mine, to bear my name before the Gentiles and kings and the sons of Israel; for *I will show him how much he must suffer for my name's sake*." In other words, suffering was simply part of Paul's apostolic calling. To be faithful to his calling, he had to embrace what Christ gave him, much suffering.

"Gave" is the right word. Because when writing to the Philippians, Paul, incredibly, calls suffering a gift, just like faith is a *gift*. "To you it has been *granted* (*echaristhë* = freely given) for Christ's sake, not only to believe in Him, but also to *suffer for His sake*" (Philippians 1:29). But this would mean that the "gift" given to him as part of his apostleship is not viewed by Paul as limited to apostles. It is "granted" to the Philippian believers, the whole church.

Others have made the same strange discovery, that suffering is a gift to be embraced. Alexander Solzhenitsyn spoke of his time in prison, with all its pain, as a gift. "It was only when I lay there on rotting prison straw that I sensed within myself the first stirrings of good. Gradually, it was disclosed to me that the line separating good and evil passes, not through states, nor between classes, nor between political parties either, but right through every human heart—and through all human hearts... Bless you, prison, for having been in my life."[2] Solzhenitsyn agrees with the apostle Paul that suffering is—or can be—a gift not just for apostles, but for every Christian.

To Show He Was Simply a Christian

Which raises the question: Did Paul, then, embrace his suffering because it would confirm that he was simply a faithful disciple of Jesus? Jesus had said, "If anyone wishes to come after me, let him deny himself, and take up his cross daily, and follow me. For whoever wishes to save his life shall lose it, but whoever loses his life for my sake, he will save it" (Luke 9:23, 24). So there is no true Christianity without cross-bearing and a *daily* dying—which sounds very much like Paul's "I die daily" (1 Corinthians 15:31). Moreover, Jesus had told his disciples, "A slave is not greater than his master. If they persecuted me, they will also persecute you" (John 15:20). So something would be amiss if Paul did not share in the sufferings of Jesus. Jesus gave his disciples an ominous image of their ministry: "Behold, I send you out as lambs in the midst of wolves" (Luke 10:3). And so he promised them, "You will be delivered up even by parents and brothers and relatives and friends, and they will put some of you to death...you will be hated by all nations on account of my name" (Luke 21:16; Matthew 24:9).

Evidently Paul did not consider these promises of suffering as limited to the original twelve apostles, because he passed them on to his churches. For example, he strengthened all his converts by telling them, "Through many tribulations we must enter the kingdom of God" (Acts 14:22). And he encouraged the suffering Thessalonian believers by exhorting them not to be "disturbed by these afflictions; for you yourselves know that we have been destined for this" (1 Thessalonians 3:3). And when he wrote to Timothy he made it a general principle: "Indeed, all who desire to live godly in Christ Jesus will be persecuted" (2 Timothy 3:12). When he spoke of his sufferings he did not treat them as unique, but said to the churches, "Be imitators of me" (1 Corinthians 4:16). So it would be understandable if Paul embraced a life of suffering because it would simply confirm that he was a Christian. "If they persecuted me, they will also persecute you."

Weaning Christians off the Breast of Self-Reliance

Since he believed that suffering was part of faithful Christian living, he probed into why this might be so. His own experience of suffering drove him deep into the ways of God's love with his children. For example, he learned that God uses our suffering to wean us from self-reliance and cast us on himself alone. After suffering in Asia he says, "We do not want you to be unaware, brethren, of our affliction which came to us in Asia, that we were burdened excessively, beyond our strength, so that we despaired even of life; indeed, we had the sentence of death within ourselves *in order that we should not trust in ourselves, but in God* who raises the dead" (2 Corinthians 1:8,9). This is God's universal purpose for all Christian suffering: more contentment in God and less satisfaction in self and the world.

I have never heard anyone say, "The really deep lessons of life have come through times of ease and comfort." But I have heard strong saints say, "Every significant advance I have ever made in grasping the depths of God's love and growing deep with him has come through suffering." Samuel Rutherford said that when he was cast into the cellars of affliction, he remembered that the great King always kept his wine there. Charles Spurgeon said that those who dive in the sea of affliction bring up rare pearls.

To Magnify Christ As a Superior Satisfaction

The pearl of greatest price is the glory of Christ. Thus Paul stresses that in our sufferings the glory of Christ's all-sufficient grace is magnified. If we rely on him in our calamity, and he sustains our "rejoicing in hope," then he is shown to be the all-satisfying God of grace and strength that he is. If we hold fast to him "when all around our soul gives way," then we show that he is more to be desired than all we have lost. Christ said to the suffering apostle, "My grace is sufficient for you, for *[my] power is perfected in weakness.*" Paul responded to this: "Gladly, then, I will boast about my weaknesses, *that the power of Christ may dwell in me.* Therefore I am content with weaknesses, with insults, with distresses, with persecutions, with difficulties, for Christ's sake; for when I am weak, then I am strong" (2 Corinthians 12:9,10). So suffering clearly is designed by God not only as a way to wean Christians off of self and on-to grace, but also as a way to spotlight that grace and make it shine. That is precisely what faith does; it magnifies Christ's future grace.

The deep things of life in God are discovered in suffering. So it was with Jesus himself. "Although he was a Son, Jesus learned obedience through what he suffered" (Hebrews 5:8). The same book where we read this also tells us Jesus never sinned (Hebrews 4:15). So "learning obedience" does not mean switching from disobedience to obedience. It means growing deeper and deeper with God in the experience of obedience. It means experiencing depths of yieldedness to God that would not have been otherwise demanded.

The Unspeakable Words of Christian Suffering

As Paul contemplated the path of his Master, he was moved to follow. But just at this point I have been astonished again by Paul's words. When he describes the relationship between Christ's sufferings and his own, he speaks what seems unspeakable. He says to the Colossian church: "Now I rejoice in my sufferings for you and I complete in my flesh what is lacking in the afflictions of Christ on behalf of his body, which is the church" (Colossians 1:24). This may be the most powerful motive for Paul's choosing a life of suffering. These words have filled me with longing for the Church of Jesus Christ. O that we would embrace the necessary suffering appointed for the advancement of Christ's kingdom in the world!

How Can We Complete the Sufferings of Christ?

What does Paul mean that he "completes what is lacking in the afflictions of Christ"? Is this an unspeakable belittling of the all-sufficient, atoning worth of the death of Jesus? Did not Jesus himself say as he died, "It is finished" (John 19:30)? Is it not true that "by one offering [Christ] *has perfected for all time* those who are sanctified" (Hebrews 10:14)? And that "through his own blood, he entered the holy place *once for all*, having obtained *eternal* redemption" (Hebrews 9:12)? Paul knew and taught that the afflictions of Christ were a complete and sufficient ground for our justification. We are "justified by his blood" (Romans 5:9). Paul taught that Christ chose suffering and was "obedient unto death" (Philippians 2:8). That obedience of suffering was the all-sufficient ground of our righteousness before God. "As through [Adam's] disobedience the many were made sinners, even so through the obedience of [Christ] the many will be made righteous" (Romans 5:19). So Paul does not mean that his sufferings complete the atoning worth of Jesus' afflictions.

There is a better interpretation. Paul's sufferings complete Christ's afflictions *not* by adding anything to their worth, but by extending them to the people they were meant to save. What is lacking in the afflictions of Christ is not that they are deficient in worth, as though they could not sufficiently cover the sins of all who believe. What is lacking is that the infinite value of Christ's afflictions is not known and trusted in the world. These afflictions and what they mean are still hidden to most peoples. And God's intention is that the mystery be revealed to all the nations. So the afflictions of Christ are "lacking" in the sense that they are not seen and known and loved among the nations. They must be carried by ministers of the word. And those ministers of the word "complete" what is lacking in the afflictions of Christ by extending them to others.

Epaphroditus Is the Key

There is a strong confirmation of this interpretation in the use of similar words in Philippians 2:30. There was a man named Epaphroditus in the church at Philippi. When the church there gathered support for Paul (perhaps money or supplies or books), they decided to send them to Paul in Rome by the hand of Epaphroditus. In his travels with this supply, Epaphroditus almost lost his life. He was sick to the point of death, but God spared him (Philippians 2:27).

So Paul tells the church in Philippi to honor Epaphroditus when he comes back (v. 29), and he explains his reason with words very similar to Colossians 1:24. He says, "He came close to death for the work of Christ, risking his life *to complete* (similar word to the one in Colossians 1:24) *what was lacking* (same word as in Colossians 1:24) in your service to me." In the Greek original the phrase *"complete what was lacking* in your service to me" is almost identical with *"complete what is lacking* in Christ's afflictions."

In what sense, then, was the service of the Philippians to Paul "lacking" and in what sense did Epaphroditus "complete" what was lacking in their service? A hundred years ago a commentator Marvin Vincent explained it like this:

> The gift to Paul was a gift of the church as a body. It was a sacrificial offering of love. What was lacking, and what would have been grateful to Paul and to the church alike, was the church's presentation of this offering in person. This was impossible, and Paul represents Epaphroditus as supplying this lack by his affectionate and zealous ministry.[3]

I think that is exactly what the same words mean in Colossians 1:24. Christ has prepared a love offering for the world by suffering and dying for sinners. It is full and lacking in nothing—except one thing, a personal presentation by Christ himself to the nations of the world. God's answer to this lack is to call the people of Christ (people like Paul) to make a personal presentation of the afflictions of Christ to the world.

In doing this we "complete what is lacking in the afflictions of Christ." We finish what they were designed for, namely, a personal presentation to the people who do not know about their infinite worth.

Filling Afflictions with Afflictions

But the most amazing thing about Colossians 1:24 is *how* Paul completes what is lacking in Christ's afflictions. He says that it is *his own sufferings* that complete Christ's afflictions. "I rejoice in *my sufferings* for you and I complete *in my flesh* what is lacking in the afflictions of Christ." This means, then, that Paul exhibits the sufferings of Christ by suffering *himself* for those he is trying to win. In *his* sufferings they see Christ's sufferings. Here is the astounding upshot: *God intends for the afflictions of Christ to be presented to the world through the afflictions of his people.* God really means for the body of Christ, the church, to experience some of the suffering he experienced so that when we proclaim the cross as the way to life, people will see the marks of the cross in us and feel the love of the cross from us. Our calling is to make the afflictions of Christ real for people by the afflictions we experience in bringing them the message of salvation.

Since Christ is no longer on the earth, he wants his body, the church, to reveal *his* suffering in *its* suffering. Since we are his body, our sufferings are his sufferings. Romanian pastor Joseph Tson put it like this: "I am an extension of Jesus Christ. When I was beaten in Romania, He suffered in my body. It is not my suffering: I only had the honor to share His sufferings."[4] Therefore our sufferings testify to the kind of love Christ has for the world.

"I Bear on My Body the Marks of Jesus"

This is why Paul spoke of his scars as the "marks of Jesus." In his wounds people could see Christ's wounds. "I bear on my body the marks of Jesus" (Galatians 6:17). The point of bearing the marks of Jesus is that Jesus might be seen and his love might work powerfully in those who see. "[We always] carry in our body the death of Jesus, so that the life of Jesus may also be manifested in our bodies. For while we live we are always being given up to death for Jesus' sake, so that the life of Jesus may be manifested in our mortal flesh. So death is at work in us, but life in you" (2 Corinthians 4:10–12).

"The Blood of the Martyrs Is Seed"

The history of the expansion of Christianity has proved that "the blood of the martyrs is seed"—the seed of new life in Christ spreading through the world. For almost three hundred years Christianity grew in soil that was wet with the blood of the martyrs. In his *History of Christian Missions*, Stephen Neil mentions the sufferings of the early Christians as one of the six main reasons the church grew so rapidly.

> Because of their dangerous situation vis-á-vis the law, Christians were almost bound to meet in secret…Every Christian knew that sooner or later he might have to testify to his faith at the cost of his life…When persecution did break out, martyrdom could be attended by the utmost possible publicity. The Roman public was hard and cruel, but it was not altogether without compassion; and there is no doubt that the attitude of the martyrs, and particularly of the young women who suffered along with the men, made a deep impression…In the earlier records what we find is calm, dignified, decorous behaviour; cool courage in the face of torment, courtesy towards enemies, and a joyful acceptance of suffering as the way appointed by the Lord to lead to his heavenly kingdom. There are a number of well-authenticated cases of conversion of pagans in the very moment of witnessing the condemnation and death of Christians; there must have been far more who received impressions that in the course of time would be turned into a living faith.[5]

"How Can I Blaspheme My King Who Saved Me?"

One example of such a powerful witness through suffering was the martyrdom of Polycarp, the Bishop of Smyrna who died in A.D. 155. His student Irenaeus said that Polycarp had been the student of the apostle John. We know he was very old when he died because, when the Proconsul commanded him to recant and curse Christ, he said, "Eighty and six years have I served him and he hath done me no wrong; how then can I blaspheme my king who saved me?"[6]

During one season of persecution a frenzied crowd in Smyrna cried out for a search to be made for Polycarp. He had moved to a town just outside the city, and three days before his death he had a dream from which he concluded, "I must needs be burned alive." So when the search was finally made, instead of fleeing he said, 'The will of God be done." The ancient account of the martyrdom gives the following record:

> So, hearing of their arrival, he came down and talked with them, while all that were present marveled at his age and constancy, and that there was so much ado about the arrest of such an old man. Then he ordered that something should be served for them to eat and drink, at that late hour, as much as they wanted. And he besought them that they should grant him an hour that he might pray freely. They gave him leave, and he stood and prayed, being so filled with the grace of God that for two hours he could not hold his peace, while they that heard were amazed, and the men repented that they had come after so venerable an old man.[7]

When he was finally taken away and condemned to burning, they tried to nail his hands to the stake, but he pled against it and said, "Let me be as I am. He that granted me to endure the fire will grant me also to remain at the pyre unmoved without being secured with nails."[8] When his body seemed not to be consumed by the fire, an executioner drove a dagger into his body. The ancient account concludes, "All the multitude marveled at the great difference between the unbelievers and the elect."[9] In large measure this is what explains the triumph of Christianity in the early centuries. They triumphed by their suffering. It did not just accompany their witness, it was the capstone of their witness. "They overcame [Satan] because of the blood of the Lamb and because of the word of their testimony, and *they did not love their life even to death*" (Revelation 12:11).

Not Till the Number of the Martyrs Is Complete

It is not a fluke of history that the church expands and is strengthened by suffering and martyrdom. This is the way God means it to be. One of the most powerful evidences that God intends to complete his saving purposes in the world by means of suffering is found in the book of Revelation. The setting is a vision of heaven where the souls of the martyrs cry out, "How long O Lord?" In other words, when will history be complete and your purposes of salvation and judgment be accomplished? The answer is ominous for all of us who want to be a part of the completion of the Great Commission. "They were told to rest a little longer, until the number of their fellow servants and their brothers should be complete, who were to be killed as they themselves had been" (Revelation 6:11).

What this means is that God has planned to complete his purposes by appointing a certain number of martyrs. When that number is complete, then the end will come. George Otis shocked many at the second Lausanne Congress on World Evangelization in Manila in 1989 when he asked, "Is our failure to thrive in Muslim countries owing to the absence of martyrs? Can a covert church grow in strength? Does a young church need martyr models?" Fittingly he concludes his book, *The Last of the Giants*, with a chapter titled "Risky Safety."

> Should the Church in politically or socially trying circumstances remain covert to avoid potential eradication by forces hostile to Christianity? Or would more open confrontation with prevailing spiritual ignorance and deprivation—even if it produced Christian martyrs—be more likely to lead to evangelistic breakthroughs? Islamic fundamentalists claim that their spiritual revolution is fueled by the blood of martyrs. Is it conceivable that Christianity's failure to thrive in the Muslim world is due to the notable absence of Christian martyrs? And can the Muslim community take seriously the claims of a Church in hiding?... The question is not whether it is wise at times to keep worship and witness discreet, but rather how long this

may continue before we are guilty of "hiding our light under a bushel...The record shows that from Jerusalem and Damascus to Ephesus and Rome, the apostles were beaten, stoned, conspired against and imprisoned for their witness. Invitations were rare, and never the basis for their missions."[10]

Otis would no doubt agree with Gregory the Great (pope from 590 to 604), when he said, "The death of the martyrs blossoms in the lives of the faithful."[11]

The Blood Flowed from Our Wounds Like a Fountain

There are countless examples in our own day of *choosing* to suffer for the purpose of Colossians 1:24—to complete what is lacking in Christ's afflictions by presenting them to others through suffering.[12] As I was writing this chapter in late 1995, a missionary letter describing such suffering came to my attention. I quickly E-mailed the missionary in Africa to confirm the facts. He spoke personally with Dansa, the man in question, and got his permission for me to quote this story in Dansa's words from the letter.

> Around 1980 there was a time of severe persecution from the local officials of the communist government in my area of Wolayta. At the time, I was working in a government office, but I was also serving as the leader of the Christian youth association for all the churches in my area. The communist officials repeatedly came to me to ask for my help in teaching the doctrines of the revolution among the youth. Many other Christians were giving in because the pressure was very great, but I could only say no.
>
> At first, their approach was positive: they offered me promotions and pay increases. But then the imprisonments began. The first two were fairly short. The third time lasted an entire year. During this time communist cadres would regularly come to brainwash the nine of us believers (six men and three women—one of whom would later become

my wife) who were being held together. But when one of the cadres converted to Christ, we were beaten and forced to haul water from long distances and carry heavy stones to clear farm land.

The worst time came during a two-week period in which the prison official would wake us early while it was still dark when no one could see and force us to walk on our bare knees over a distance of up to 1.5 kilometers on the gravel road of the town. It would take us about three hours. After the first day, the blood flowed from our wounds like a fountain, but we felt nothing.

On another occasion one particularly brutal prison official forced us to lie on our backs under the blazing sun for six straight hours. I don't know why I said it, but when we finished I told him, "You caused the sun's rays to strike us, but God will strike you." A short time later, the official contracted severe diabetes and died.

When the communist government fell several years later, the head official invited us back to preach in the jail. At that time, twelve prisoners being held for murder received Christ. We have continued to minister in the prison, and there are now 170 believers. Most of the prison officials have also believed.

Only God can sort out all the influences that led to this remarkable time of harvest among the prison inmates and officials. But surely it would be naive to think that the suffering of Dansa was not part of the compelling presentation of the reality of Christ in the lives of those who believed.

Demoted for Christ and for Salvation

Joseph Tson has thought deeply about the issue of suffering for Christ as a way to show Christ to the world. He was the pastor of the Second Baptist Church of Oradea, Romania, until 1981 when he was exiled by the government. I have heard him interpret Colossians 1:24 by saying that Christ's suffering is for *propitiation*, our suffering is for *propagation*. He points out that not only Colossians 1:24, but also 2 Timothy 2:10 makes suffering the means of evangelism: "I endure all things of the sake of the elect, so that they may obtain the salvation which is in Jesus Christ." According to Joseph Tson, Paul is saying,

> If I had remained a pastor in Antioch, in that affluent and peaceful city, in that wonderful church with so many prophets and such great blessings, nobody in Asia Minor or Europe would have been saved. In order for them to be saved, I have had to accept being beaten with rods, scourged, stoned, treated as the scum of the earth, becoming a walking death. But when I walk like this, wounded and bleeding, people see the love of God, people hear the message of the cross, and they are saved. If we stay in the safety of our affluent churches and we do not accept the cross, others may not be saved. How many are not saved because we don't accept the cross?[13]

He illustrates how the very suffering of Christians itself is what often provides the means of fruitful evangelism.

> I had a man in an important position whom I baptized come to me and ask, "Now what shall I do? They will convene three or four thousand people to expose me and mock me. They will give me five minutes to defend myself. How should I do it?"
>
> "Brother," I told him, "defending yourself is the only thing you shouldn't do. This is your unique chance to tell them who you were before, and what Jesus made of you; who Jesus is, and what he is for you now."
>
> His face shone and he said, "Brother Joseph, I know what I am going to do." And he did it well—so well that afterwards he was severely demoted. He lost almost half of his salary. But he kept coming to me after that saying, "Brother Joseph, you know I cannot walk in that factory now without someone coming up to me. Wherever I go, somebody pulls me in a corner, looks around to see that nobody sees him talking to me, and then whispers, 'Give me the address of your church,' or 'Tell me more about Jesus,' or 'Do you have a Bible for me?'"

Every kind of suffering can become a ministry for other people's salvation.[14]

Choosing to Suffer for the Sake of the Nations

I conclude, then, that when Paul said, "If for this life only we have hoped in Christ, we are of all men most to be pitied," he meant that Christianity means choosing and embracing a life of suffering for Christ that would be pitiable if Christ proved false. Christianity is not a life that one would embrace as abundant and satisfying without the hope of fellowship with Christ in the resurrection. And what we have seen is that this embracing of suffering is not just an accompaniment of our witness to Christ, it is the visible expression of it. Our sufferings make Christ's sufferings known, so that people can see the kind of love Christ offers. We complete Christ's afflictions by providing what they do not have, namely, a personal, vivid presentation to those who did not see Christ suffer in person.

The startling implication of this is that the saving purposes of Christ among the nations and in our neighborhoods will not be accomplished unless Christians choose to suffer. At the extreme end of this suffering, the number of martyrs is not yet complete (Revelation 6:11). Without them, the final frontiers of world evangelization will not be crossed. Less extreme is the simple costliness in time and convenience and money and effort to replace excessive and addictive leisure with acts of servant love: "Let your light so shine that men may see your good deeds and give glory to your Father in heaven" (Matthew 5:16).

But Is This Christian Hedonism?

I have titled this chapter "Suffering: the Sacrifice of Christian Hedonism" even though [elsewhere] I quoted David Livingstone as saying that the sufferings of his missionary service were not a "sacrifice." This is not a contradiction or a disagreement with Livingstone. Words are like that. Context is almost everything. When he says suffering is not a sacrifice, he means th blessings outweigh the losses. When I say that suffering is a sacrifice, I mean that there are losses—great losses. When you realize that I agree with Livingstone, it simply implies that I see the blessings as massive.

But I am going to retain the use of the word sacrifice. The pain is too great, the losses too real to pretend that we can only talk in terms of no-sacrifice. We must simply keep our definitions clear.

My answer is, Yes, this is Christian Hedonism. The entire New Testament treats suffering in a Christian Hedonist context.

Was Paul pursuing deep and lasting joy when he chose suffering—so much suffering that his life would have been utterly foolish and pitiable if there were no resurrection from the dead? The question virtually answers itself. If it is the resurrection alone that makes Paul's painful life-choices *not* pitiable but praiseworthy (and possible!), then it is precisely his hope and quest for that resurrection that sustains and empowers his suffering. This is, in fact, exactly what he says: he counts all ordinary human privileges as loss "that I may know [Christ] and the power of his resurrection and the fellowship of his sufferings, being conformed to his death; *in order that I may attain to the resurrection from the dead*" (Philippians 3:10,11). His aim is to so live—and suffer—that he is assured of resurrection from the dead.

Giving All to Gain Christ

Why? Because resurrection meant full, bodily, eternal fellowship with Christ. That was the center of Paul's hope: "I count [all things] but rubbish in order that I may gain Christ" (Philippians 3:8). Gaining Christ was Paul's great passion and goal in all he did. "To live is Christ and to die is gain" (Philippians 1:21). Gain! Gain! This is the goal of his life and suffering. Paul "desired to depart and be with Christ, for that is *very much better*" (Philippians 1:23). "Very much better" is not an altruistic motive. It is a Christian Hedonist motive. Paul wanted what would bring the deepest and most lasting satisfaction to his life, namely, being with Christ in glory.

But not alone with Christ in glory!

No one who knows and loves Christ can be content to come to him alone. The apex of his glory is this: "You were slain, and purchased for God, with your blood, persons from every tribe and tongue and people and nation" (Revelation 5:9). If this is the summit of Christ's glorious mercy, then those who count it their infinite gain, cannot live for private pleasures. The pleasures at Christ's right hand are public pleasures, shared pleasures, communal pleasures. When Paul said that he counted everything as loss in order to gain Christ, his losses were all for the sake of bringing others with him to Christ. "If I am to be poured upon the sacrifice and service of *your faith*, I rejoice, indeed I rejoice with you all" (Philippians 2:17). The pouring out of his life in sufferings was, to be sure, "that he might gain Christ," but it was also that he might gain *the faith* of the nations that magnifies the mercy of Christ.

My Joy, My Crown of Exultation!

This is why Paul called the people he had won to faith *his joy*. "My loved brothers, my desired ones, *my joy* and crown, so stand firm in the Lord, my loved ones" (Philippians 4:1). "Who is our hope or *joy* or crown of exultation? Is it not even you, in the presence of our Lord Jesus at His coming? For you are our glory and *joy*" (1 Thessalonians 2:19,20). The church was his joy because in their joy in Christ his joy in Christ was greater. More of Christ's mercy was magnified in multiplied converts of the cross. So when Paul chose suffering in the cause of world evangelization and said that his aim was to "gain Christ," he meant that his own personal enjoyment of fellowship with Christ would be eternally greater because of the great assembly of the redeemed enjoying Christ with him.

Even though I am not as far along as Paul was in his passionate love for the church, I thank God that there have been key points in my life where God has rescued me from the pit of cynicism. I recall the days as I was finishing college and starting seminary. The mood in the late sixties was inhospitable to the local church. I can remember walking the streets of Pasadena on Sunday mornings in the fall of 1968, wondering if there was any future for the church—like a fish doubting the worth of water, or a bird wondering about the reason for wind and air. It was a precious work of grace that God rescued me from that folly and gave me a home with the people of God at Lake Avenue Church for three years, and let me see in the heart of Ray Ortlund, my pastor, a man who exuded the spirit of Paul when he looked out on his flock and said, "My joy, my crown of exultation."

Ten years later there was another moment of crisis as I stood at my table late at night in October of 1979 writing in my journal. The issue was, would I remain as a professor at Bethel College teaching Biblical Studies, or would I resign and look for a pastorate? One of the things God was doing in those days was giving me a deeper love for the church—the gathered, growing, ministering body of people that meet week in and week out and move into the likeness of Christ. Teaching had its joys. It is a great calling. But that night another passion triumphed, and God led me, over the next months, to Bethlehem Baptist Church. As I write these words, it has been over fifteen years. If I allow myself, the tears come fairly easily when I think about what these people mean to me. They know, I hope, that my great passion is to "gain Christ." And unless I am mistaken, they also know that I live for "the advancement and joy of their faith" (Philippians 1:25). It is the aim of my writing and preaching to show that these two aims are one. I gain more of Christ in one converted sinner and growing saint than in a hundred ordinary chores. To say that Christ is my joy and Bethlehem is my joy is not double talk.

If Joy in Suffering Is Admirable, Pursue It

It should not surprise us, even though it is utterly unnatural, that Paul should say in Colossians 1:24, "I *rejoice* in my sufferings for you and I complete in my flesh what is lacking in the afflictions of Christ." In other words, when I complete Christ's afflictions by making a personal presentation of them to you in my own afflictions and pain, I rejoice. I rejoice.

Christian Hedonism simply says this is a good and admirable thing that Paul is doing, and we should go and do likewise. To treat this magnificent spiritual event of joy in suffering as something small or incidental or not-to-be-pursued is close to blasphemy. I say this carefully. When the Holy Spirit himself does such a great thing, and thus magnifies the all-sufficiency of Christ in suffering, it is close to blasphemy to say, "It is permissible to experience suffering for others, but not to pursue the joy." The Christ-exalting miracle is not just the suffering, but the joy in suffering. And we are meant to pursue it. In 1 Thessalonians 1:6,7 Paul says, "You...received the word in much tribulation with the *joy of the Holy Spirit*, so that you *became an example* to all the believers in Macedonia and in Achaia." Notice two crucial things: First, joy in tribulation is the work of the Holy Spirit; second, it is an example for others to follow. Beware of those who belittle the miracles of the Spirit of God by saying they are good gifts but not good goals.

Rejoice in Persecution, Your Reward Is Great!

Christian Hedonism says that there are different ways to rejoice in suffering as a Christian. All of them are to be pursued as an expression of the all-sufficient, all-satisfying grace of God. One way is expressed by Jesus in Matthew 5:11,12. "Blessed are you when men cast insults at you, and persecute you, and say all kinds of evil against you falsely, on account of me. *Rejoice, and be glad, for your reward in heaven is great*" (cf. Luke 6:22,23). One way of rejoicing in suffering comes from fixing our minds firmly on the greatness of the reward that will come to us in the resurrection. The effect of this kind of focus is to make our present pain seem small by comparison to what is coming. "I consider that the sufferings of this present time are not worthy to be compared with the glory that is to be revealed to us" (Romans 8:18; cf. 2 Corinthians 4:16–18). In making the suffering tolerable, rejoicing over our reward will also make love possible, as we saw in chapter four. "Love your enemies and do good, expecting nothing in return; and *your reward will be great*" (Luke 6:35). Be generous with the poor "and you will be blessed, since they do not have the means to repay you; for *you will be repaid at the resurrection of the just*" (Luke 14:14).

Rejoice in Affliction, It Deepens Assurance!

Another way of rejoicing in suffering comes from the effects of suffering on our assurance of hope. Joy in affliction is rooted in the hope of resurrection, but our experience of suffering also deepens the root of that hope. For example, Paul says, "We exult in our afflictions, knowing that affliction produces endurance, and endurance produces proven genuineness, and genuineness produces hope" (Romans 5:3,4). Here Paul's joy is not merely rooted in his great reward, but in the effect of suffering to solidify his hope in that reward. Afflictions produce endurance and endurance produces a sense that our faith is real and genuine, and that strengthens our hope that we will indeed gain Christ.

Richard Wurmbrand describes how one may survive the moments of excruciating pain of torture for Christ.

> You have been so much tortured, nothing counts any more. If nothing counts any more, my survival doesn't count either. If nothing counts any more, the fact that I should not have pain also does not count. Draw this last conclusion at the stage at which you have arrived and you will see that you will overcome this moment of crisis. If you have overcome this one moment of crisis, it gives you an intense inner joy. You feel that Christ has been with you in that decisive moment.[15]

The "intense joy" comes from the sense that you endured with the help of Christ. You have been proven in the fire and you have come through as genuine. You did not recant. Christ is real in your life. He is for you the all-satisfying God that he claims to be. This is what the apostles seemed to experience according to Acts 5:41 when, after being beaten, "they went on their way from the presence of the Council, *rejoicing that they had been considered worthy to suffer shame for his name.*" The joy came from the thought that their faith was regarded by God as real and ready to be proved in the fire of affliction.

Rejoice in Suffering with Christ, It Leads to Glory!

Another way of rejoicing in suffering is kindled by the truth that our joy itself is a proven pathway to glory. Joy in suffering comes not only 1) from focusing on our reward, and 2) from the solidifying effect of suffering on our sense of genuineness, but also 3) from the promise that joy in suffering will secure eternal joy in the future. The apostle Peter expresses it like this: "To the degree that you share the sufferings of Christ, keep on rejoicing; *so that* also at the revelation of his glory, you may rejoice with exultation" (1 Peter 4:13). Joy now in suffering is the appointed pathway to the final rejoicing at the revelation of Christ. Peter is calling us to pursue joy now in suffering (he commands it!) so that we will be found among those who rejoice exceedingly at the coming of Christ.

Rejoice in Suffering for Others, They See Christ!

The fourth way of rejoicing in suffering we have seen already. It comes from realizing that through our suffering others are seeing the worth of Christ and standing firm because of our faith in the fire. Paul says to the Thessalonians, "Now we really live, if you stand firm in the Lord. For what thanks can we render to God for you in return for *all the joy with which we rejoice because of You before our God*" (1 Thessalonians 3:8,9). This is the joy of Colossians 1:24, "I rejoice in my sufferings for you."

When we suffer to show others the love of Christ and the worth of Christ, it is because every new convert that stands firm in faith is a new, unique prism for refracting the all-satisfying glory of Christ. The joy we feel in them is not a different joy than we feel in Christ. The glory of Christ is our "great gain." For this we will suffer the loss of anything and everything. And everyone who sees in our suffering the superior worth of Christ, and believes, is another image and evidence of that great worth —and therefore another reason to rejoice.

The Happiest People in the World

The Calvary road with Jesus is not a joyless road. It is a painful one, but it is a profoundly happy one. When we choose the fleeting pleasures of comfort and security over the sacrifices and sufferings of missions and evangelism and ministry and love, we choose against joy. We reject the spring whose waters never fail (Isaiah 58:11). The happiest people in the world are the people who experience the mystery of "Christ in them, the hope of glory" (Colossians 1:27), satisfying their deep longings and freeing them to extend the afflictions of Christ through their own sufferings to the world.

God is calling us to live for the sake of Christ and to do that through suffering. Christ chose suffering; it didn't just happen to him. He chose it as the way to create and perfect the church. Now he calls us to choose suffering. That is, he calls us to take up our cross and follow him on the Calvary road and deny our-selves and make sacrifices for the sake of ministering to the church and presenting his sufferings to the world.

Brother Andrew, who heads a ministry called Open Doors and who is most famous for his 1967 book, *God's Smuggler*, describes Christ's call in the mid 1990s like this:

> There's not one door in the world closed where you want to witness for Jesus…Show me a closed door and I will tell you how you can get in. I won't however, promise you a way to get out…

Jesus didn't say, "Go if the doors are open," because they weren't. He didn't say, "Go if you have an invitation or a red carpet treatment." He said, "Go," because people needed his Word...

We need a new approach to missions—an aggressive, experimental, evangelical, no-holds-barred approach...a pioneering spirit...

I'm afraid we'll have to go through a deep valley of need and threatening situations, blood baths; but we'll get there.

God will take away what hinders us if we mean business. If we say, "Lord, at any cost..."—and people should never pray that unless they truly want God to take them at their word—he will answer. Which is scary. But we have to go through the process. This is how it has worked in the Bible for the last two thousand years.

So we face potentially hard times, and we have to go through that...We play church and we play Christianity. And we aren't even aware we are lukewarm...We should have to pay a price for our faith. Read 2 Timothy 3:12: "Indeed, all who want to live a godly life in Christ Jesus will be persecuted." The church has been much purified in countries where there was a lot of pressure...All I can say is to be ready. [16]

Not to Prove Our Power but His Preciousness

The answer to this call is a radical step of Christian Hedonism. We do not choose suffering simply because we are told to, but because the one who tells us to describes it as the path to everlasting joy. He beckons us into the obedience of suffering not to demonstrate the strength of our devotion to duty, nor to reveal the vigor of our moral resolve, nor to prove the heights of our tolerance for pain; but rather to manifest, in childlike faith, the infinite preciousness of his all-satisfying promises. Moses "*chose* to share ill-treatment with the people of God rather than enjoy the fleeting pleasures of sin...because he looked to the reward" (Hebrews 11:25,26). Therefore his obedience glorified the God of grace, not the resolve to suffer.

The Essence of Christian Hedonism

This is the essence of Christian Hedonism. In the pursuit of joy through suffering, we magnify the all-satisfying worth of the Source of our joy. God himself shines as the brightness at the end of our tunnel of pain. If we do not communicate that he is the goal and the ground of our joy in suffering, then the very meaning of our suffering will be lost. The meaning is this: God is gain. God is gain. God is gain.

The chief end of man is to glorify God. And it is more true in suffering than anywhere else that *God is most glorified in us when we are most satisfied in him.* My prayer, therefore, is that the Holy Spirit would pour out on his people around the world a passion for the supremacy of God in all things. And I pray that he would make it plain that the pursuit of joy in God, whatever the pain, is a powerful testimony to God's supreme and all-satisfying worth. And so may it come to pass, as we "complete what is lacking in Christ's afflictions," that all the peoples of the world will see the love of Christ and magnify his grace in the gladness of faith.

Notes

1. Richard Wurmbrand, *Reaching Toward the Heights* (Bartlesville, OK: Living Sacrifice Book, 1992), back cover.

2. Quoted by Philip Yancey in "Frozen Fire," *Christianity Today*, October 5, 1984, p. 109.

3. Marvin Vincent, I.C.C., *Epistle to the Philippians and to Philemon* (Edinburgh: T. & T. Clark, 1897), p. 78.

4. Jospeh Tson, "A Theology of Martyrdom," an undated booklet of The Romanian Missionary Society, P.O. Box 527, Wheaton, IL, 60189-057, p. 4.

5. Stephen Neil, *A History of Christian Missions* (Harmondsworth, Middlesex: Penguin Books Ltd., 1964), pp. 43,44.

6. Quoted in "The Martyrdom of Polycarp," in *Documents of the Christian Church*, Henry Bettenson, ed., (London: Oxford University Press, 1967), p. 10.

7. "The Martyrdom of Polycarp," pp. 9,10.

8. "The Martyrdom of Polycarp," p. 11.

9. "The Martyrdom of Polycarp," p. 12.

10. George Otis, Jr., *The Last of the Giants: Lifting the Veil on Islam and the End Times* (Grand Rapids: Chosen Books, 1991), pp. 261,263.

11. Quoted in Joseph Tson, "A Theology of Martyrdom," p. 1.

12. See the examples in John Piper's *Let the Nations Be Glad: The Supremacy of God in Missions* (Grand Rapids: The Baker Book House, 1993), pp. 94–96. See almost any of the books by Richard Wurmbrand, for example, *Tortured for Christ* or *If That Were Christ, Would You Give Him Your Blanket?* or *Victorious Faith.* Other sources include *Called to Suffer, Called to Triumph* by Herbert Schlossberg and *God Reigns in China* by Leslie Lyall.

13. Joseph Tson, "A Theology of Martyrdom," p. 2.

14. "A Theology of Martyrdom," p. 3.

15. Richard Wurmbrand, "Preparing for the Underground Church," in *Epiphany Journal*, Vol. 5, No. 4, Summer, 1985, p. 50.

16. Brother Andrew, "God's Smuggler Confesses," an interview with Michael Maudlin in *Christianity Today*, December 11, 1995, p. 46.

For the Joy Set Before Us

Helpful Resources from Desiring God Ministries

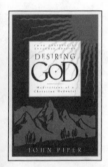

Desiring God
Meditations of a Christian Hedonist
John Piper
$9.00 (retail $12.99)

The great business of life is to glorify God by enjoying Him forever. Discord between duty and delight doesn't exist: delight is our duty. Piper stuns us again and again with things we saw in the Bible, but never dared to believe. Join him on this dangerous quest for maximum joy in God. But beware, it may cost you your life. Never mind—"the steadfast love of the Lord is better than life" (Psalm 63:3). This 10th anniversary edition includes: new Preface, expanded Introduction, revised chapters 1 & 2, updated chapter 9 on Missions, all-new Chapter 10 on Suffering, and Study Guide.

Desiring God Ministries

DGM is a resource ministry of Bethlehem Baptist Church in Minneapolis, Minnesota. We exist to help you make God your treasure. We have produced hundreds of resources for this purpose. Most of our inventory consists of books and audiotapes by Dr. John Piper. In addition, we also produce God-centered children's curricula, host conferences, and coordinate John Piper's conference speaking schedule. Ask us about our "whatever you can afford" policy. Contact us for a free resource catalog:

(888) 346-4700   www.desiringgod.org

Let The Nations Be Glad!
The Supremacy of God in Missions
John Piper
$9.00 (retail $12.99)

This book is a call to the Church to catch a God-centered vision for engaging in world evangelization. Piper shows that worship is the ultimate goal of the church, and that this God-centered worship fuels missions. He devotes chapters to such issues as worship, prayer, suffering, Universalism and annihilationism, God's sovereignty and evangelism, and unreached peoples.

The Pursuit of Joy Through Suffering

This is the essense of what we call Christian Hedonism: In the pursuit of joy through suffering, we magnify the all-satisfying worth of the Source of our joy. God himself shines as the brightness at the end of our tunnel of pain. If we do not communicate that he is the goal and the ground of our joy in suffering, then the very meaning of our suffering will be lost. The meaning is this: God is gain. God is gain. God is gain.

The chief end of man is to glorify God. And it is more true in suffering than anywhere else that *God is most glorified in us when we are most satisfied in him.* Our prayer, therefore, it that the Holy Spirit would pour out on his people around the world a passion for the supremacy of God in all things. And we pray that he would make it plain that the pursuit of joy in God, whatever the pain, is a powerful testimony of God's supreme and all-satisfying worth.

(Adapted from *Desiring God: Meditations of a Christian Hedonist, 10th Anniversary Expanded Edition* (Sisters, OR: Multnomah Books, 1996), p. 238.)

Desiring God Ministries
720 Thirteenth Avenue South
Minneapolis, MN 55415-1793
888-346-4700
612-373-0651 International
612-338-4372 Fax
mail@desiringgod.org
www.desiringgod.org

God is most glorified in us when we are most satisfied in Him.

Persecution Outlines

for Study and Presentation

Milton Martin

Edited and revised. Used by permission of
Milton Martin Missionary Ministries.

Milton Martin Missionary Ministries
P.O. Box 1567
Route 2, Box 2624
Belton, TX 76513
(254) 933-9339

The Church Functioning
(Matthew 16:18)

I.   Christ founded His Church and commissioned her to carry on His work. (Matthew 16:18; 28:18–20)
  A. If our buildings are ever closed, will this mean the end of our Christianity?
  B. The first Churches did not have Temples or buildings.

II. The first church was persecuted severely! How did they respond?
  A. They met in private homes. (Acts 5:42)
  B. "Lay Christians" faithfully shared their testimony. (Acts 8:1,4)
  C. They took advantage of every opportunity to witness and testify. (Acts 16:12,13)
  D. They taught disciples. (Acts 11:25,26)
  E. They fellowshipped together while ministering. (Acts 2:46,47)
  F. They worshipped under every circumstance and opportunity. (Acts 16:23–25)

III. Alternative means of worship, fellowship and witness were observed.
  A. House churches were prevalent. (Romans 16:3–5; 1 Corinthians 16:19)
  B. Persecuted Christians and "unregistered" churches use birthdays, weddings and funerals as opportunities to meet as a body.
  C. Can you suggest some forms and ways?

IV. Some means that Satan uses to defeat Christians and churches during persecution.
  A. Satan uses isolation as a tool against churches.
  B. Satan uses guilt and offenses as a weapon against churches.
      1. The Devil is the "accuser of the brethren."

2. The accusations of Satan are continuous and never ending.

3. The evil one watchfully waits to pounce when sin has not been confessed.

4. Much care has to be taken to continually maintain communion and fellowship with the Lord. (1 John 1:8–10)

5. Personal offenses not confronted become very serious and can grow into "mountainous" problems.

6. Satan does his best to cause Christians to carry "false guilt" after sin has been forgiven. (Romans 5:1,2; 8:33,34)

7. Instead of doubting and asking, "Why?" say, "Lord, what would you have me to do?"

Christians Will Suffer Presecution
(1 Peter 4:12–19)

I. Promise of Suffering. (1 Peter 2:21; 4:12; 1 Thessalonians 3:3,4; Acts 14:22; 2 Timothy 3:12; Mark 13:9,13; Philippians 1:29)

II. Purpose of Suffering. (1 Peter 4:12; "Fiery trial." Job 23:10; Psalm 66:10)
   A. Proof of our faith.
   B. When something is professed, it is necessary to prove it's reality.
   C. Proof of the depth of our faith.
      1. What will it take to move us or cause us to turn aside?
      2. The importance or size of that which hinders reveals the strength of our faith.

III. Participation With Christ in His Sufferings. (1 Peter 4:13) Literally the Christian enters into the sufferings of Christ. It will not be the cross but it may be at the hands of men.
   A. The Lord was denied. (John 1:10,11)

    B. The Lord was hated. (John 15:24; Isaiah 53:3)

    C. The Lord left the comfortable house of His Father. (John 3:16)

    D. The Lord did not have a house of His own.

    E. The Lord did not have the money even to pay His taxes. (Matthew 17:27)

    F. The Lord did not have a bed.

    G. The Lord had no one to defend Him when He was falsely accused. (1 Peter 2:22,23)

    H. The Lord had no tomb. (Isaiah 53:9)

    I. The Lord became poor.

    J. Philippians 3:10; 1 Peter 2:21; 4:1; Galatians 2:20; 6:12,17; Acts 5:41; Hebrews 12:2; 1 Thessalonians 2:2.

What will be our reaction? (Hebrews 12:2)

IV. Power in Suffering or Through Suffering. (1 Peter 4:14) The Holy Spirit rests upon those who suffer. In the Old Testament a cloud was a symbol of the presence of God. This cloud was known as the glory of the Lord (1 Kings 8:10,11). A similar glory comes on a believer by the Holy Spirit when he suffers for Christ. The Spirit comes to minister—to fill, to cover, to clothe, to enclose, to sustain, to help, to strengthen, to intercede, and to make up that which is lacking. This glory was seen in Stephen (Acts 6:5–8; 7:55,60). The darker the night, the brighter the stars (2 Corinthians 12:9,10).

V. Dangers in Suffering. (1 Peter 4:14–16)

    A. There is a difference in suffering for Christ and suffering for one's own guilt or foolishness.

    B. Shame. (Hebrews 2:11)

    C. Bitterness instead of joy and thanksgiving. (Exodus 15:23,24; 16:2; 1 Thessalonians 5:16–18)

VI. Purification Through Suffering. (1 Peter 1:7; 4:12)

    A. Suffering can be used to purify, purge, burn up "dross."

    B. Suffering in itself cannot refine or purify. Only the

grace of God can produce refining and purification, but suffering can cause us to recognize our need.

1. Suffering can help us understand that nothing can be done in our strength.
2. Suffering can make us sensitive to sin.

C. Through suffering we can learn to completely depend upon the Lord. (2 Corinthians 12:9,10)
D. How will we respond? Entrust our souls to God. (1 Peter 4:19; Acts 7:59; Luke 23:46)

The Part of Suffering in the Life of the Believer

Suffering is common to every person (Job 5:6,7). It is normal for a Christian to suffer as well (2 Timothy 3:12; Acts 14:22; 1 Peter 2:21).

There are levels of persecution: pressure, humiliation, discrimination, threats, loss of material possessions or physical violence.

I. Common Misconceptions.
   A. Suffering is punishment for some wrong or sin. (1 Peter 4:19; 3:14; 4:16)
   B. Thinking that one should never be sad. (1 Peter 1:6)
   C. Thinking that only Christians suffer. (Genesis 3:16–19)
   D. Unhealthy enchantment with suffering.
   E. Unreasonable fear of suffering.

II. What the Bible Teaches About Suffering.
   A. Christians are to expect suffering. (John 15:18–21; 17:14; 1 John 3:13)
   B. Suffering can be the will of God for us. (1 Peter 4:16; 2:21)
   C. Suffering in the life of the child of God has a purpose. (1 Peter 1:6,7; 2 Corinthians 12:7–10)
   D. We should suffer for righteousness' sake. (Matthew 5:10; 1 Peter 4:15)
   E. God blesses right suffering. (Matthew 5:10–12; Luke 6:22,23)

F.   Suffering causes us to look to heaven. (Romans 8:16–18; Colossians 3:1–3)

G.   We should not be ashamed or embarrassed about suffering. (1 Peter 4:16; Hebrews 13:12,13)

H.   We must follow the example of Christ. (1 Peter 2:19–25)

I.   We must react under suffering as the Lord did. (Matthew 5:38–48; Romans 12:14,17–21; 1 Peter 2:21–23)

J.   We can have the victory. (John 16:33)

III. Prepare for Suffering.

A.   Understand it to be normal. (1 Peter 4:12; Philippians 1:29)

B.   Know the teaching of the Word of God. (Philemon 3:10; Romans 6:3–5; John 8:31,32)

C.   Abide in Christ. (John 15:4)

D.   Submit daily to the Holy Spirit. (Ephesians 5:18; 4:30)

E.   Rest in the will of God. (Ephesians 5:17; Hebrews 4:1,9–11)

F.   Edify your brethren when you and they are suffering. (Colossians 3:16,17; Ephesians 5:19–21)

Ways Attack May Come to Churches

I.   The Focus of Persecution. (John 15:18–21; Colossians 1:24–27)

The attack has been and always will be against our Lord.

II. The Language of the Overcomer.

A.   The rallying words of a conqueror—"overcome." (Revelation 2:7,11,17,26; 3:5,12,21)

B.   The secret of overcoming. (Revelation 12:11)

1.   "By the blood of the Lamb." (Revelation 12:11a) (Note study on importance of the blood.)

a.   Peace with God

b.   Peace with our conscience.

c.   Power in the life.

d.   This weapon is lost:

       1) By liberal theology—no blood.

       2) By liberation theology—no cross.

       3) By burdenless preaching—no power.

2. "By the word of their testimony." (Revelation 12:11b)

   a. Satan attempts to rob us of the victory by causing us to not open our mouth or causing us to lose our testimony and credibility.

   b. There is the "internal enemy" also.

       1) Division within congregations.

       2) Fear.

       3) Unbelief.

       4) Lack of love.

       5) Sidetracked on issues, etc., rather than focusing on people and souls.

   c. Lack of care of our families.

   d. Plans and projects that are not the will of God.

   e. Anything that would put our life out of balance.

3. "They loved not their lives unto the death." (Revelation 12:11c)

   a. Compromise is not in the vocabulary.

   b. Examples of Christians who have suffered.

   c. Not only the physical life is involved. It may be necessary to die to ambitions, position, and rights.

III. General Signs.

Persecution is not some kind of a blanket or exact, detailed thing in every country, be it Communist, religious or some other totalitarian government. There are some general signs, however, when persecution may begin.

A. Limitations in evangelism.

   1. Christians are not given permission to travel or choose their employment.

   2. All Christian programs are eliminated from radio and TV.

3. Any religious meetings outside of church buildings are prohibited.
4. Permission must be secured for the times of worship. No meeting together except at those specified times.
5. Government infiltrators or spies are present in all services.

B. The importation of Bibles and Christian literature is prohibited.
   1. Such printed material is considered non-essential.
   2. There are situations where the Bible was placed in the same category as pornographic material.

C. Foreign missionaries are expelled from the country.
   1. By laws limiting clergy to local nationals.
   2. By laws prohibiting foreigners to work in the country. In others, one can only be a tourist with limited stay or travel only in certain specified areas.
   3. By direct threats and violence against foreigners.

D. Christian leaders are threatened and severely discriminated against.
   1. Mail is censored and pastors are limited in the subjects they can preach.
      a. Tax-exempt status will be taken from the churches if anything political is even mentioned from the pulpits.
      b. Pastors are kept "in line" by threats of the seizing of their children by the government.
   2. Pastors are not allowed to devote all their time to the ministry.
      a. "They must become productive members of the society." This means that they must become bi-vocational.
      b. They may be assigned to such jobs that take all their strength and time.
   3. Pastors are not allowed to visit their members or to distribute gospel literature

4. Churches are not allowed to have typewriters, computers or printing equipment.

5. Pastors may be manipulated by scare tactics.

   a. They may be summoned for questioning.

   b. They may be forced to attend certain government "indoctrination" classes.

   c. Special "tempting" offers may be made to them as coercion or seduction.

     1) This may be in the form of special privileges.

     2) It may be in the form of admission of their children into college or to other vocations rather than those to which Christians are limited.

   d. They may be harassed by unannounced house searches.

   e. Their services may be invaded by a number of government officials.

6. Pastors may be assigned to work in some remote and distant place in the country.

   a. The purpose is to isolate them from their people and other Christians.

   b. They may be given very demeaning and humiliating jobs.

7. Pastors are arrested and "re-educated."

   a. This can include torture.

   b. They may be put to open shame.

   c. False accusation and untrue testimony given against them.

E. Churches are forced to register.

  1. All church leaders must be approved by the state.

  2. All sermons must be written out and reviewed by certain individuals or departments before they can be delivered.

  3. Statements must be signed before pastors are allowed to preach. (Example: "No attempt will be

made to evangelize the unsaved.")

F. Denominations are forced to unite.
1. The number of denominations is limited.
2. All come under the control of a national ecumenical council.
3. A totally national church is "created."

G. Educational and vocational opportunities for Christians are limited.
1. Only members of certain youth groups are allowed to attend university.
2. No Christian can be a doctor, lawyer, professor or social worker.
3. Christians have no choice in their vocation or employment.

H. Religious education of all under 18 is prohibited.
1. Home schooling is not allowed.
2. Christian young people are forced to attend "special education" classes on atheism, evolution, sex education and "alternate lifestyles."
3. Parents who violate the law are subject to the loss of their children.

I. Christians are prohibited from giving aid to each other. When one member of a family is arrested, the family loses certain "rights" or "privileges."
1. This may include the right to medical care, housing or food.
2. The family is isolated by not being allowed to fraternize with fellow believers or even other extended family members.

J. Churches are closed.
1. Buildings are converted to other uses.
2. Christians are "assigned" to remote or other areas so as to isolate them.
3. Christians are forbidden to have contact with other believers.

IV. Many Christians Firmly Believe That It Will Never Happen to Them.
  A. For some reason they believe themselves exempt.
  B. Although there are different interpretations about the "rapture," this is not an escape clause. We have no right to believe that God will excuse us from persecution.

V. Present Lessons for Believers.
  A. Pray as never before for our nation and its leaders. (1 Timothy 2:1–4; Romans 13:1–7)
  B. Determine to be a conqueror for Christ. (Revelation 12:11)

Some Possible Forms That Persecution May Take
(1 Peter 2:19–24)

Suffering is a part of the life of every true believer. There are at least 33 possible ways that one may suffer.

1. For righteousness' sake. (Matthew 5:10; 1 Peter 3:14)

2. By slander (evil report). (Psalm 31:13; Job 19:18; 55:12–14; Luke 6:22)

3. Shame. Open embarrassment, dishonor or disgrace. Manner in which our Lord was accused of being conceived, born out-of-wedlock; also, manner in which His nakedness was openly displayed on the cross. (Hebrews 13:13; 11:26)

4. Falsely accused. (Psalm 35:11; 27:12; Matthew 5:11; Luke 23:2,5,10; Mark 14:55–60; Acts 6:13; 16:19–23; 26:2,7)

5. Ensnare through deceit, trapping, tricks, seeking ways to accuse. (Daniel 6:4,5; Luke 11:54; Matthew 10:16–18)

6. Object of conspiracy. (2 Samuel 15:12; Genesis 37:18; 2 Corinthians 11:32; Acts 9:23)

7. Mocked (Psalm 42:3)—to scorn, to scoff, to sneer, to make a play of. (Job 12:4; Matthew 27:29,31,41; Acts 2:13; 17:18,32; Hebrews 11:36)

8. Betrayed—treated treacherously. (Matthew 24:10; Luke 21:16; Psalm 41:9)

9. Despised—to have contempt for, to loathe, to think nothing of, to consider without honor. (1 Corinthians 1:28; 4:10c)

10. Hated by family. (Matthew 10:21,34–36; Micah 7:6; Luke 21:16)

11. Hated by men. (Luke 21:17; Matthew 10:22; Job 19:19)

12. Defamation of character, libel, slander, evil report. (Psalm 31:13; Job 19:19; 1 Peter 2:12; 1 Corinthians 4:13)

13. Feared by own people. (Acts 9:26)

14. Subject to special trials. (1 Corinthians 4:9–14; 2 Corinthians 11:23–28)

15. Imprisoned. (Luke 21:12; Acts 4:3; 5:18; 12:4; 16:24; 2 Corinthians 6:5; 11:23c; Hebrews 11:36b)

16. Beaten. (Acts 5:40; 16:23; 2 Corinthians 6:5; 11:24; Matthew 10:17)

17. Contradicting. (Acts 13:45)

18. Stir against. (Acts 6:12; 13:50; 14:2,19; 19:23,25,26, 29; 21:27)

19. Press charges before authorities. (Acts 18:12; Matthew 10:17,18)

20. Threatened. (Acts 4:18,21; 5:40)

21. Stoned. (Acts 7:58,59; 14:19; 2 Corinthians 11:25; Hebrews 11:37)

22. Afflictions. (2 Timothy 3;11; Psalm 34:19)

23. Expulsion. (Acts 13:50; John 16:2a)

24. Exhaustion, extreme fatigue. (2 Corinthians 11:27)

25. Hunger and thirst. (2 Corinthians 11:27; 1 Corinthians 4:11)

26. Spectacle. (1 Corinthians 4:9; Acts 9:16; 20:23; 21:11; Hebrews 10:33a)

27. Suffer physical need. (1 Corinthians 4:11; 2 Corinthians 6:4; Philippians 4:12; Hebrews 11:37)

28. Martyrdom. (Luke 21:16; Acts 7:59; 12:2; John 16:2)

29. Afflictions. (2 Timothy 1:8; 4:5; Matthew 24:9; Psalm 34:19; 2 Corinthians 4:17; 6:4; Hebrews 10:32,33; 11:25,37; Colossians 1:24; 1 Thessalonians 1:6; 3,7; James 5:10)

30. Poverty. (2 Corinthians 6:10; Philippians 4:12)

31. Loss of property and material goods. (Hebrews 10:34b)

Some Necessities for Overcoming Through Persecution

I. Select and Disciple Spiritual Leaders According to the New Testament. (Acts 14:21,22; Titus 1:5)
   A. Leaders were not proud because of their position. (1 Timothy 3:6; 1 Peter 5:3)
   B. Leaders were true servants. (1 Peter 5:2; John 13:14–17)
   C. Leaders identified with the people.
   D. Leaders were men of integrity and honesty, recognized not just by Christians but by all.
   E. Leaders possessed special valor and courage that enabled them to remain true.

II. Take Time to Disciple. (2 Timothy 2:2)
   A. Select a limited number of God-chosen people to disciple. (Luke 6:12)
   B. Spend time with your disciples. (Mark 3:14)
   C. Teach them by example. (1 Corinthians 4:15,16; Philippians 4:9; John 13:14–17)
   D. Give simple, clear instructions. (Acts 20:26,27)
   E. Inspect assignments.
   F. Teach them accountability and build character. (1 Timothy 4:12–16)
   G. Intercede for them specifically by name daily. (Ephesians 1:16; Philippians 1:3–6; Colossians 1:3)

III. Our Families Must Be Protected.
   A. Make sure that each member is saved and that Christ is Lord. (Colossians 1:9–13; 2 Corinthians 13:5; Romans 8:1–14)

B. Prepare each of our children for the storm clouds that will come upon them. (Deuteronomy 6:4–9,20–25; 11:18–21; 30:2; Proverbs 6:20–24; Joshua 24:14,15)

C. Collect Scriptures and Christian material which is always accessible to the family.

D. Never forget to share with the less fortunate. (Romans 12:9–18; 13:8; 15:1; 1 Corinthians 16:1; Acts 20:35; Galatians 6:2)

IV. Look for Alternative Ways and Methods to Carry on and Continue Witnessing for Christ. (Matthew 16:18)

A. Keep the youth active and involved.

B. Learn everything possible about others' suffering and visit them. (Hebrews 13:3)

C. Show genuine love by caring for all, especially in times of need; for example, food, care, sharing during times of illness, special need, deaths. (Matthew 25:35–40; 5:43–45; James 1:27; 2 Timothy 1:16–18; Romans 12:20)

D. Guard against all bitterness. (Romans 12:14,17,19,21; Matthew 5:38–48)

E. Do not repay evil with evil. (Matthew 5:44; Luke 23:34; Acts 7:60; 1 Corinthians 4:11–13; 1 Peter 2:23)

F. Pray for your enemies. (Matthew 5:44)

The Night Cometh, When No Man Can Work
(John 9:4)

Regardless of claims being made, there are still over 40 nations "closed" to the preaching of the gospel. Other countries are in great danger of losing religious freedom and liberties. What about the souls in these countries? Jeremiah 8:20 is their cry and dilemma. We must "work the works of Him—while it is day" (John 9:4).

I. Considering the Words of Christ.

A. What can be meant by the word "night"? The absence

of Christ somewhere or anywhere is equivalent to "night" (darkness—absence of light).

1. When people oppose the gospel and the cause of Christ, it is "night." (Mark 5:17)
2. When religion becomes inflamed with passion, rage, and attacks God, it is "night." Christ was crucified by religious Jews. (Matthew 27:20–25)
3. When sin is allowed in the believer's life, unconfessed and not forsaken, it is "night." (1 John 1:5,6)
4. When Christ comes back for His own, "eternal night" will have arrived for many. (Matthew 24:30,31)

B. What can be meant by the word "work"?

1. Obedience to the will of God is to "work the works of Him." (John 9:4)
2. When we allow Christ to work in and through us— this is to "work the works of Him." (Matthew 5:15,16)

II. How Is the Night Coming When No One Can Work?

A. The powers of darkness are working to bring darkness into the world and more specifically to certain areas. (Ephesians 5:11; 6:12)

Their methods are: Secular humanism, new age, worship of political powers, false cults, amorality and perversion.

B. Satan sows seeds of darkness in hearts, churches and society. (Matthew 13:24–28)

III. Why Would the Night Come When No One Will Be Able to Work?

A. It is a natural law that night comes after the day.

B. We live in a vast field of wickedness and the Bible reveals that evil will grow worse and worse. (2 Timothy 3:13)

C. Diminished light and cold, weak Christians will not affect this world. (Matthew 6:22,23; 5:13–15; Revelation 3:15,16)

D. During times of spiritual darkness, sin is not seen as sin nor is error viewed as error (times of no absolutes and self and situational ethics reigning). (2 Timothy 3:1–9; 4:3,4)

IV. What Must We Do?
   A. Take advantage of the light of the day.
      1. We must enter whether doors are open or "closed." (We must get the gospel to the greatest number of people possible with the most effective means possible in the least possible time.)
      2. Discern the ripe fields of the world. (The Spirit of God prepares hearts in certain areas at special times.)
      3. Know "open and tolerant" areas and take advantage of preparation for the gospel by certain circumstances; for example, Paul going to synagogues first in each city and building on their understanding of God and the Scriptures. (Acts 13:5,14,15; 17:1–3; 18:2,4; 19:8)
      4. Beat the cults and "isms" to new mission fields.
   B. Do not trade the pure gospel for cultural or social religion or simply a church building.
   C. It is time to act! (African proverb: "Run while the sun is hot.")
      1. Let us give ourselves to fasting and prayer, truly seeking the Lord. (Isaiah 55:6,7; Psalm 32:6,7)
      2. We must sanctify ourselves and renounce all known sin. (Isaiah 1:16,17; Jeremiah 4:14; Romans 12:9; John 17:17)
      3. Walk in the Spirit and win souls. (Romans 13:13; Galatians 5:25; Ephesians 4:1; 5:15,16; Colossians 1:10; Philippians 2:14–16)

Turning Trials Into Triumphs
(James 1:2–12)

Popular preaching and teaching proclaims that the Christian life is without problems.

However, looking at it biblically, one finds that God is the author of "strange ministries." Through these ministries God causes all things to work together for good (Romans 8:28). Blessings can be wrapped in the rags of a curse. Sorrow is a disguise that real joy wears. Through trials, affliction, and suffering, God desires to accomplish something otherwise not possible in our lives. God never wastes time and never wastes experiences —if we will but respond correctly. God is sovereign. God wills it and, except it be because of sin and chastisement, the Christian must consider trials and suffering as natural and normal.

The difference in being happy or being unhappy is not the absence of trouble and problems. The difference lies in what you do with it.

Two Ways to React To Trials

1. God's way—accomplishes many things for good.
2. World's way—reaction of carnality, which results in resentment, bitterness and premature death.

Recognize that circumstances are not just chance: God is in control.

1. They are of God.
2. They are good.

God Wills That:

1. Trials be turned to triumph.
2. Victims become victors.
3. Crosses become crowns.
4. Suffering is to become glory.
5. Battle is to be the means of victory.

James 1:2 – Count
    1:3 – Know
    1:4,9 – Let
    1:5,6 – Ask

Four Essentials for Victory Over Trials
1. Joyful attitude (v. 2)
2. Understanding the purpose (v. 3)
3. A surrendered will (v. 4)
4. A heart that wants to believe (v. 6–8)

I. Count It All Joy: A Joyful Attitude. (James 1:2)
    A. Outlook determines outcome. Attitude will determine action.
    B. Trials are to be expected. (v. 2; 1 Peter 4:12)
    C. "When ye fall into divers temptations." (v. 2b) Various and varicolored. (Example: Like a quilter sews together blocks of fabric to make a blanket. Look at it on the back, it seems to be only faded colors, rough, nothing visible to appreciate—a mess. Look at the front, the side intended to be viewed—the pattern, design, beauty and purpose is seen.) So God arranges and blends experiences and happenings in our lives so that faith may be exercised and grow.
    D. Values determine evaluations.
        1. If one values comfort more than character, trials will not be allowed to accomplish the purpose of God.
        2. If one values the material and physical more than spiritual, you will be miserable during testings.
        3. If one values for the present, rather than the future, trials will produce bitterness rather than betterment.

II. Know: Understanding the Purpose. (James 1:3)
    A. Faith is always tested. If it is not being tested, maybe it is a sign that there has never been saving faith.
    B. God tested Abraham in order to bless and to increase

his faith through exercise.
1. God tests to bring out the best.
2. Satan tests and tempts to bring out the worst.
C. Testing works for us, not against us. (Romans 8:28)
D. Trials rightly used help us to mature. (Romans 5:3,4)
1. Purpose, patience, endurance, preparation, perseverance, enablement (get up, get started, continue, keep on going, finish the race).
2. Patience is not a passive, fatalistic acceptance of circumstances. It is courageous perseverance in the face of suffering and difficulty.
3. Impatience and unbelief always go together. (Hebrews 6:12; 10:36; Isaiah 28:16)

III. Let: A Surrendered Will. (James 1:4)
God cannot work in us without our consent. If we encounter trials without surrendered wills, we will behave as spoiled, rotten, selfish, self-centered, immature children.

IV. Ask: A Heart That Wants to Believe. (James 1:5,6)
A. What should we pray for? Wisdom. (Why not grace or strength?)
B. Knowledge is information. Wisdom is applied knowledge.
C. We need wisdom so we will not waste the opportunities God gives for our good, for our growth and for His glory.
D. God allows things to come to build us up. Satan uses things to tear us down.

Combatting Doubt and Worry
(Philippians 4:7; Galatians 3:23; 1 Peter 1:5)

1. Let the peace of God be as an overflowing fountain or spring in your heart and life. (Philippians 4:7)
2. Renounce all doubt and worry. (Philippians 4:6; James 4:7)
3. Guard your thoughts; think on the pure and correct. (Phil-

ippians 4:8)

4. Focus your mind and eyes on the Lord and the things of God. (Isaiah 26:3; Colossians 3:1–3; Matthew 6:33)

5. Use supernatural weapons in all supernatural warfare. (2 Corinthians 10:4–6)

6. Put on all the armor of God. (Ephesians 6:10–18)

7. Walk in faith! (Matthew 6:25–34; 7:7–11; 17:20; 21:22; Mark 11:22–24)

8. Walk in the Spirit. (Galatians 5:16–26; Romans 6:14–23; 8:1–13)

9. Keep your confidence only in God. (Hebrews 3:6,12–14; 6:11,12; 10:19–23,35–39)

10. Cast all cares and concerns on the Lord. (1 Peter 5:7)

Rewards for Christian Suffering
(1 Peter 4:13)

1. Glory in heaven. (2 Corinthians 4:17,18; 1 Peter 5:1,10,11)

2. Eternal consolation. (2 Corinthians 1:7; Romans 8:17)

3. Christ is made known. (2 Corinthians 4:11)

4. Life is being given to others. (2 Corinthians 4:12)

5. Grace of God is being made manifest. (2 Corinthians 4:15)

6. A guarantee that God will judge righteously. (2 Thessalonians 1:4,5)

7. Will reign with him. (2 Timothy 2:12a)

8. Spirit of glory rests upon. (1 Peter 4:14)

9. Glory is brought to God. (1 Peter 4:16)

10. Reason for joy. (1 Peter 4:13,14)

Sevenfold Example of Christ in Suffering
(1 Peter 2:21–24; 3:14–17)

1. Sufferings. (1 Peter 2:21; Matthew 16:24; 1 John 2:6)

2. Sinlessness. (1 Peter 2:22; Isaiah 53:9)

3. Guilelessness (1 Peter 2:22); Deceit.

4. Love when being mocked. (1 Peter 2:23; Isaiah 53:7; Romans 5:3; 12:14; Matthew 5:44–48; James 1:2–4)

5. Patience in threatenings. (1 Peter 2:23; Romans 12:12; Luke 21:19)

6. Resignation to God. (1 Peter 2:23; 4:19; Luke 23:46). Committed His cause; trusted it to God.

7. Righteousness (1 Peter 2:24); Just, Unbiased, Impartial.

Some Lessons on Preparation for Persecution: Counsel to Servants and Slaves
Biblical Admonition to Employees and Workers

Ephesians 6:5–8; Colossians 3:22–25

1. Obey master in everything. (Ephesians 6:5; Colossians 3:22)

2. Responsible—with fear and trembling. (Ephesians 6:5; Colossians 3:22)
   In all things—fearing God
   (Not choosing our likes or dislikes; not choosing to do pleasant things and rejecting unpleasant things.)

3. Not serving to be seen. (Ephesians 6:6a; Colossians 3:22c)

4. Doing the will of God. (Ephesians 6:6c; Colossians 3:22c)

5. From the heart. (Ephesians 6:6d; Colossians 3:22d) Wholeheartily.

6. With good will—gladly and joyfully. (Ephesians 6:7)

7. If not recognized by men, will be recognized by the Lord. (Ephesians 6:8; Colossians 3:24,25) The Lord will reward. (Galatians 6:7–9)

Titus 2:9,10

1. Be obedient to master. (Titus 2:9a) Please well in all things. (Titus 2:9b)

2. Not answering back. (Titus 2:9c) Not contradicting; not putting the other person in bad light.

3. Not purloining. (Titus 2:10) Not stealing or defrauding; not robbing time nor quality of workmanship. (Luke 16:10) Showing good fidelity. Faithful in all things, both large and small. (Luke 16:10)

1 Peter 2:18–20

1. Be subject. (1 Peter 2:18a) Submit, accountable to, answerable to, dependent upon, responsible to, bound by, controlled by or under the control of, under the thumb of another.

2. With all fear. (1 Peter 2:18b) Having respect to or recognizing the position of another.

3. Suffer wrongfully. (1 Peter 2:19,20) With patience; not deliberate martyrdom or suffering.

4. Follow the example of Christ. (1 Peter 2:21–23) Called to follow in the steps of Christ.

The Spiritual Nature of Our Battle
(Ephesians 6:12; 2 Corinthians 10:3,4)

The victory is ours through Christ (Romans 8:32,37; 1 Corinthians 15:57). It is true that around the world there are many battles, apparent defeats, set-backs, closed doors, spiritual failure and yes, deaths. However, below are some principles that we can keep in mind to encourage us:

I.   God is still sovereign and in control. (Isaiah 40:15; Daniel 2:20–22; 4:35; Job 12:14–23; Psalm 75:6,7; 76:10; Jeremiah 27:5–7; Proverbs 1:24–31; Hebrews 13:8)

II. God has never failed in His promises. (2 Corinthians 1:20; 2 Peter 1:4)
     There are over seven thousand promises in the Bible—one for every need of the believer. (Joshua 21:45; 23:14; 1 Kings 8:56; Hebrews 6:13–18; Acts 7:5; 2 Peter 3:9. Related promises: Hebrews 2:3; Isaiah 30:18; Psalm 34:8; Proverbs 16:20; Jeremiah 17:7,8)

III. Victory is assured because of the Lord's mandates.

With each commandment that the Lord gives, He gives sufficient grace to fulfill or carry it out to completion. (2 Corinthians 9:8; 12:9; Ephesians 3:20)

To the obedient church, the Lord has promised:

A. His power—Authority (Matthew 28:18)
B. His presence (Matthew 28:20)
C. His provision (Philippians 4:13–19)

IV. Victory is also based in the Lord's coming. (2 Thessalonians 2:8)

In glory with His own. (Revelation 1:5–8; 19:11–16; Philippians 2:9–11; Ephesians 1:19–22; Romans 16:18; Isaiah 11:3–5; Job 4:3–9; Psalm 91:14–16)

It Will Never Happen Here

1. How did the people react to Noah's message? (Matthew 24:37–39)

2. What did Peter say when Jesus told him that He would suffer and die soon? (Matthew 16:21,22)

3. How did Jesus react to this? (Matthew 16:23)

4. What did Jesus say on another occasion about His coming suffering? (Matthew 26:31)

5. How did Peter react? (Matthew 26:33–35)

6. What happened when this actually took place? (Matthew 26:69–75)

7. Why did Peter deny his faith?

8. Was the situation unique in the case of Peter?

9. Can you quote other examples where people were faced with the same choice?

From the Bible:

From somewhere in our world:

10. What does 1 Thessalonians 5:3 say about people who believe nothing can disrupt their security?

11. Peter had to learn this in his own life with Christ. Explain something of this example. (Matthew 14:29–31)

12. By allowing himself to be led by circumstances, Lot made the wrong choice.

    A. What choice was this? (Genesis 13:10,11)

    B. What was the result? (Genesis 19:15–26)

    C. Why did Lot never think about the impending destruction of Sodom and Gomorrah?

    D. How did sons-in-law react? (Genesis 19:14)

13. What happened unexpectedly to the rich man in the parable told by Jesus? (Luke 12:16–21)

14. What does the Lord say we must do in times of disaster and persecution? (Luke 21:8–28)

Biblical Principles of Persecution

1. According to John 15:18–21, what is the reason for Christian persecution?

2. How were the disciples strengthened by Paul and Barnabas? (Acts 14:22)

3. Against whom was the persecution actually directed? (Acts 9:4,5)

4. According to 2 Timothy 3:12, is persecution unlikely, likely, or inevitable?

5. Give some reasons why many Christians forsake Christ. (Matthew 13:20,21)

6. What three things does Christ expect from us in Matthew 16:24?

7. What three things does the Lord promise to those who are prepared to be persecuted? (Matthew 5:10–12)

8. God's promises are almost always preceded by a condition. Example: Revelation 3:20.

   What is the condition?

   What is the promise?

9. Name at least three similar texts.

10. Which condition precedes the promise God gave to Israel in Deuteronomy 11:22?

11. When can we depend on God's promises for:

    A. Peace (Isaiah 26:3)

    B. Political stability (1 Timothy 2:1–3)

12. What should our attitude be towards those who persecute us?

    A. Matthew 5:44

    B. Luke 23:34

13. What were Peter and John's reactions when they were beaten for their faith? (Acts 5:41)

14. What was the context of the disciples' prayer when they were persecuted? (Acts 4:23–30)

15. What type of suffering is mentioned in Romans 8:35–39?

16. What does the Bible say about victory in Romans 8:31–39?

17. Name at least three verses which indicate that all Christians will be persecuted.

18. Although strife and persecution will increase, victory is a certainty. Why?

    Do you have verse(s) to prove this?

19. What must each Christian do to be able to overcome personally? (Ephesians 6:10–18)

20. Which part of the armor is lacking most in your own personal life?

21. Would you like to bring about a change? Specify.

22. In Revelation 12:11, three ways to overcome Satan are mentioned. What are they?

The Voice of the Martyrs *Free* Subscription Offer!

The Voice of the Martyrs has been actively serving the persecuted church since 1967. Our mission is clear. With the continual persecution of Christians around the world, we strive to bring practical and spiritual assistance while making their voice heard.

Our faith can often seem incomplete without the knowledge and testimonies of our persecuted brothers and sisters. They are living examples of uncompromising faith, serving as pure evidence of God's love and faithfulness despite the surrounding obstacles.

We invite you to request a *free* subscription to *The Voice of the Martyrs* newsletter. Each month you will be encouraged as you read testimonies of persecuted Christians. You will learn to pray specifically for those who suffer for Christ. *The Voice of the Martyrs* newsletter also provides practical suggestions on ways you can be involved. Don't miss out on this opportunity to fellowship with this unique part of the Body of Christ.

The Voice of the Martyrs also has available many other books, videos, brochures, and other products to help you learn more about the persecuted church. In the U.S., to request a resource catalog, order materials, or receive our free monthly newsletter, call (800) 747-0085 or write to:

> The Voice of the Martyrs
> P.O. Box 443
> Bartlesville, OK 74005-0443
> E-mail: thevoice@vom-usa.org
> Visit our website at www.persecution.com

If you are in Canada, the United Kingdom, Australia, New Zealand, or South Africa, contact:

The Voice of the Martyrs
P.O. Box 117
Port Credit
Mississauga, Ontario L5G 4L5
Canada
Website: www.persecution.net

Release International
P.O. Box 54
Orpington BR5 9RT
United Kingdom
Website: www.releaseinternational.org

Voice of the Martyrs
P.O. Box 250
Lawson NSW 2783
Australia
Website: www.persecution.com.au

Voice of the Martyrs
P.O. Box 8452
Papanui, Christchurch 8005
New Zealand

Christian Mission International
P.O. Box 7157
1417 Primrose Hill
South Africa

FOXE: Voices of the Martyrs

John Foxe's *Book of Martyrs* has been cherished around the world for centuries by Christians who have been inspired by the faithful witness of those who paid the ultimate price for their testimony of Jesus Christ. The Voice of the Martyrs is now releasing an updated version, including accounts from 33 A.D. through 2006.

Read the accounts of modern martyrs, such as Ghorban from Iran who died in 2005, and despite threats said, "I am not going to deny Jesus and return to Islam." A week later, Ghorban was dead. Three men murdered the Iranian Christian, stabbing him in the street. When Ghorban's wife discovered his body, a crowd gathered around. She cried, "O people, remember that Ghorban is a Christian martyr who laid down his life for the sake of Christ!" Though Ghorban's family has been under extreme pressure to turn back to Islam, his wife and children say they will follow Jesus no matter what the cost.

There are many more testimonies of martyrs like Ghorban. Their stories will inspire you as you follow Jesus. Each book includes a unique copper-plated cross made of four nails symbolizing the heroic faith of Christian martyrs and VOM's commitment to remember those who are currently persecuted for their faith in Jesus Christ.

Between Two Tigers

In Vietnam, some tigers have four feet. Others have only two feet. Vietnamese Christians courageously spread the gospel between the government tiger and the religious tiger. A Vietnamese rice farmer shares,

"I try to carry little Bible tracts with me and one Bible. I would rather carry the literature than food, so I don't bring food

with me. Sometimes we run into wild animals. We can hear the voice and see the footprints of the tigers. There are many snakes. The people follow witchcraft and animism; they worship the plants and rocks. When we are walking on the trail, we pray constantly. We are not scared of the jungle, but we are scared of the Vietnamese border police. If we meet them along the way, they will shoot us ... But my favorite Bible verse is, 'Go and make disciples of all the nations.'"

As you walk with these brothers and sisters between their tigers, you will become renewed and strengthened with a modern-day view of those who are called "Christians."

Tortured for Christ

Months of solitary confinement, years of periodic physical torture, constant suffering from hunger and cold, the anguish of brainwashing and mental cruelty—these are the experiences of a Romanian pastor during his fourteen years in Communist prisons.

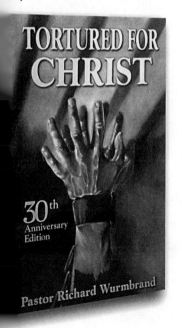

Richard Wurmbrand's "crime," like that of thousands of others, was his fervent belief in Jesus Christ and his public witness concerning that faith.

Meeting in homes, in basements, and in woods—sometime daring to preach in public on street corners—these faithful souls persisted in their Christian witness knowing full well the ultimate cost of their actions.

This is their story—a classic account of courage, tenacious faith, and unbelievable endurance. This history of the Underground Church reflects the continuing struggle in many parts of the world today.

Read the book that launched the ministry of The Voice of the Martyrs in the founder's own words.

Extreme Devotion

Are you up for a challenge? Read 365 true accounts of men and women who totally sold out for Christ. See if it isn't unlike any other devotional you've ever read.

Serious followers of Jesus pay a price, and extreme followers often pay the ultimate price. The Voice of the Martyrs, coauthors of the bestseller *Jesus Freaks*, brings you a daily

devotional filled with stories of courage, commitment, confession, and compassion—a price demanded; a price paid.

In an age of extremes, you can find faith, strength, encouragement, and hope through the stories of fellow believers from all over the world, from centuries past up to the present. These men and women, both young and old, went to the outer limits of human devotion.

Each story is true. Each story is unforgettable. Each story is extreme. Each story will change your life.

Take the challenge today and see for yourself.

Hearts of Fire

"Either you marry or you die... If you are a Christian, then there is no place for you in this city... you will die here alone."

Tara's father's parting words brought only one thought to the mind of the sixteen-year-old girl—she must escape for her life. Beaten to the brink of death, Tara—the daughter of a prominent Pakistani Muslim—was locked in her room as a prisoner without food or medical attention.

All because she was caught with a Bible.

Tara's story is not unique among these eight courageous women in *Hearts of Fire*. From the young Vietnamese girl who turns down freedom in order to evangelize the people of her Communist homeland, to the Australian missionary who spreads the message of forgiveness and healing across India after her husband and sons are burned alive by the village zealots, these women have overcome extreme adversity to emerge as leaders and ministers in the underground church around the world.

The Voice of the Martyrs brings you the true stories of courageous women, heroines of the faith, who are representatives of countless women facing similar situations around the world. These role models of faith and passion will inspire you to pursue Christ with heart aflame, no matter what the cost.

Notes